IN THE PRESENCE OF MY ENEMIES

IN THE PRESENCE

W · W · NORTON & COMPANY · INC ·

NEW YORK

OF MY ENEMIES

John W. Clifford, s.j.

TO MY FATHER AND MOTHER—
MODELS OF DEDICATION, SELF-SACRIFICE,
AND CHEERFUL COURAGE.

Contents

Foreword

THIS IS A BOOK I HAD TO WRITE—AS AN AMERICAN. For many years I have been disturbed by the impact of communist psychological warfare on the United States. In particular, I have been appalled by the reaction to the tactic of brainwashing, as applied to captured American prisoners in the Orient. In many instances I have heard this technique described with awe as a new mystique, against which there is no defense.

It is neither mysterious nor irresistible. I know. I know because I lived through three years of the most intense brainwashing in the jails of Shanghai. I learned how the communists can be defeated at their own game. I discovered also that the captive who fights the communists with uncompromising dedication to his cause not only can survive but will emerge from imprisonment stronger than those who seek favors through collaboration.

My experiences, in fact, confirm the conclusions of army psychiatrists who studied the cases of American war prisoners captured in Korea. The doctors said, in effect, that silence, strict noncooperation and a tough determination to hang onto his own dignity could save the prisoner; and that nothing else could. This was proved at the time by the 18 per cent of Korean War captives who refused all collaboration and who survived far better than their less resolute comrades. Since then the lesson seems to have been forgotten and, unfortunately, a number of books on the subject have tended to spread defeatism.

Now, with the involvement of U.S. forces in guerrilla warfare in Southeast Asia, we read once again about young Americans being subjected to this intense psychological warfare. I have decided, therefore, to write an analysis of my experiences, with the hope that it may dispel the mystery of brainwashing and, perhaps, give strength to the new soldiers who may experience it and to the loved ones waiting for them at home.

The tragedy of the American prisoners in Korea who gave comfort to the enemy is not what they did under pressure. The real tragedy is that these men were totally unprepared for what they had to undergo. I believe, very firmly, that any normal strong personality, when properly trained and motivated, can overcome communist measures completely.

There is some disagreement among experts over the proper name for this communist technique, but there is general agreement that the purpose is to break a man's will completely. When it was first used against them, in the early days of communist control, the Chinese of Shanghai called it "hsi-nao"—"wash the brain." So I shall call it brainwashing. In the sense that I use it, the technique is not designed to make communists of its victims but to turn them into soulless robots available for complete manipulation.

This is not an academic subject. Nor is it limited to soldiers or their anxious relatives. Every American is involved in the war against the communists. To know the individual communist at his worst is to be forewarned against mass efforts to spread international intimidation.

Individual communists appear in this book, and so do their jails and their cities—and some of the stanch Chinese who opposed them. But this is not primarily a personal experience story. My purpose is to dissect and explore the technique and theory of brainwashing, using my experiences as illustration. I hope to show how this tactic can be defeated by any spirited man encountering it. The techniques which I shall describe remain standard for all communists, not only for the Chinese.

I am a rather ordinary American, from a typical middle-class home. When arrested in Shanghai in 1953 I had only vicarious experience with deep suffering and my greatest fear had been of the dentist's drill. My only preparation for the ordeal ahead was seven years' work among the Chinese of Shanghai and a knowledge of the Mandarin language. These were useful, but not essential, for my fight against the communists. At my release, in 1956, I had not submitted a confession nor given my captors a single fragmentary sentence of propaganda value. They freed me, even though at the last minute I refused to sign the papers they insisted were necessary. In other words, I behaved like a normal, stubborn American—and that is what saved me. The fact that I am also a Jesuit missionary is beside the point; any strong-willed man could have done the same.

PART ONE

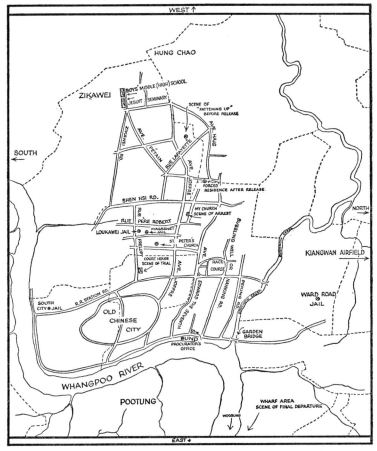

ROUGH SKETCH OF SHANGHAI SHOWING PRINCIPAL LANDMARKS AND APPROXIMATE LOCATIONS OF EVENTS TOLD IN BOOK

Chapter one

SHANGHAI
AT THE START OF THE
KOREAN WAR

SOLDIERS FILLED THE STREET—THE IN-
tense, tight-lipped soldiers of the communist People's
Republic of China. Several thousand of them marched in
cadenced obedience down Avenue Joffre, a little slice of Paris
in Shanghai. As they marched, they shouted virulent anti-
American slogans with screaming hoarseness and chanted
communist songs. The front ranks carried large signs, proclaiming that the "People's Liberation Army" was prepared
to save the fatherland from "American invasion." This was
July, 1950, a month after the start of the Korean War, and
Peiping already was trying to whip its people into military
fever.

As the soldiers roared toward us, the sweating Chinese
driver steered my pedicab toward a curb. He slammed his

bare feet on the hot asphalt, in place of brakes, and our vehicle lurched to a halt. I bounced forward in the seat, clutching a mountainous pile of diagrams and charts which I was carrying for a lecture at a summer school for Chinese Catholic students. Although the communists had controlled the city for nearly fourteen months, my notebooks were filled with material to counteract their false propaganda. For the last several months I had tried to prove to my students by innuendo and double-talk that their newly trimphant government was lying to them. Now, I thought ironically, I was loaded with explosives, if any of the grim soldiers marching toward us was able to read my notes—or my mind.

The driver cowered protectively over the rusty frame of the pedicab, a cross between a bicycle and a ricksha. I could do nothing but sit in the broiling sun and guess at the probable reaction when these slogan-drunk young soldiers spotted a foreign priest. They were dressed for battle, with rifles and ammunition belts and swaying hand grenades. Although they were regulars, these young, beardless farm boys looked more like fresh recruits than veterans of China's long civil war. Nevertheless, this was the first military display I had seen since the start of Korean hostilities, and it seemed more foreboding than the usual communist demonstrations, which had become almost commonplace.

The column drew up to us, still screaming, still half running, a khaki dragon. The soldiers evidently had been turned out as a show of power, to excite the city or to awaken it. But the curbs were empty, and none in the swirling crowds of Chinese on the sidewalks paid any attention. They were more interested in the food stores and the chic shops, for which Avenue Joffre was famous, now open again for business after the first uncertainties of communist occupation. So this element of the People's Liberation Army jogged onward unnoticed. For an instant we were alone in the vacated street—

the army, a lone Catholic priest, and a very frightened pedicab boy.

The front ranks of the column cascaded past me without
stopping. They were pointed toward the towering modern
skyline of the city built by foreigners, more than a century
before, on a deserted mud flat on the banks of the Whangpoo
River. Now the skyline and the city belonged to the Chinese
and, as a foreigner, I was there only by sufferance. But, if
they guessed the irony of the moment, none of the soldiers
reacted to it. As the troops swelled around the pedicab, it
seemed for an instant as if I had become part of an anti-
American parade in Asia's largest communist city. Despite
the slogans, however, there was no sign of hostility on their
strained faces; no sign, in fact, that they recognized the "foreign devil" in their midst. Only one looked up momentarily
at me, and his pockmarked face merely showed a flicker of
surprise, with no animosity.

I remembered this little incident long afterward. When
the communists finally threw me into jail and began their
systematic attempts to break me, the interrogators repeated
one consistent theme. They would scream "imperialist" at
me at every opportunity, shouting that all the Chinese people
were determined to liquidate my kind. But their own soldiers
had proved the opposite, that hot Shanghai day, by hurrying
past me without a hostile gesture. To the communists, however, everyone who opposed them was an "imperialist," if
he were foreign, and a "spy" or a "counterrevolutionary," if
Chinese. There was, in their minds, no alternative.

This was not the China to which I had come four years
before. As a young seminarian, fresh from the quiet sun-
baked hills of California, I was deposited without ceremony
in the breathless anthill of postwar Shanghai. Nothing in my
normal, rather sheltered American life had prepared me for
that first encounter with clamorous China. Living as a youth

in San Francisco, I had felt the tug of the Orient which had magnetized many thousands of others, and I had been honed by the internationalism of the Pacific city.

But still I was a raw American, more eager than prepared. The shock of my introduction to Shanghai was unforgettable —the roaring streets, choked with traffic; the endless thousands of rushing people, and the noise. Standing in amazement on the Bund that first day, I laughed and thought of my mother. She was continually referring to my brother and me as noisemakers. I only wished she had been with me to see and hear real noisemakers.

Then I recalled how she had stood on the pier, with my father, my brother and sister-in-law, as my ship pulled away from San Francisco. She was crying, and so were the rest of us. Ours always had been a close-knit family, my father and mother and one brother, two years older than I. Once before I had seen my mother cry, when I had announced that I was going to be a priest. She had been both happy and sad, knowing that I would leave home permanently.

Both my parents were born in San Francisco. Except for a trip to Southern California, where my dad had taken a job, we had traveled little. Money was not abundant. When work became scarce in Southern California, we had returned to San Francisco, and as soon as I was able I helped out. I remembered canvassing the neighborhood for lawn-mowing jobs and frequently being told: "You're too small." Several people let me try, however, and I proved to them that I could.

The crash of a brass gong brought me back to Shanghai. It was loud enough to summon ghosts and, I learned later, it was a traditional Chinese method of advertising everything from a bowl of noodles to an opera. The clamor seemed to intensify as I watched the street drama, and I thought I never would become accustomed to the noise.

Everyone was talking when I arrived, and they continued

14

to talk until the communists eventually silenced them—the men shouting, the women screaming, the children giggling. Shanghai in those days bubbled with the effervescent good humor which had protected the Chinese from a thousand great plagues, of man and nature. How was anyone to know that the greatest plague of all was on the way.

A short time later, I was sent to the old capital of Peiping * to study Mandarin. There, China captured me forever. Nodding drowsily in the northern sun, Peiping clutched the past, like an old man holding a rare book, and all the greatness of this ancient and massive country shone around the city. This was Peiping's Indian summer of history—the period between the unmourned departure of the Japanese conquerors and the arrival of the communist conquerors. The civil war already had begun up in the north, and much of the nation was in turmoil. But the old city was more interested in contemplating its temples. In quiet solitude I was able to pursue my studies, living with Chinese seminarians and drawing patient kindliness and dignity from them. In long walks through the dusty, tree-bordered city I discovered the lovableness of the simple Chinese people; strangers who would stop to talk and joke with me, correcting my faltering Chinese. Most of all, perhaps, I remember the laughter of cherubic children and the day of triumph when I first understood what they were saying in Chinese. These people endeared themselves to me at once.

When I returned to Shanghai in September, 1947, to continue theological studies, uncertainty over the future already gripped the city. I was assigned to the seminary in Zikawei, a section of the former French Concession. Our rather exten-

* Peiping, "northern peace," was the name used for this city at the time of my arrival in China. The communists have reestablished the capital there and use the classical name Peking, meaning "northern capital." Both names refer to the same city, the cultural center of old China. The Chinese Nationalists still use Peiping.

sive compound included the church, two seminaries, a boys' and a girls' high school, each with more than one thousand students. I plunged energetically into my work as a student of both Chinese and theology and, eventually, as a priest, after my ordination in June, 1950. But almost from the beginning it seemed as if my efforts were foredoomed. The Chinese communists had begun the military campaign which carried them inexorably across the continent and, finally, into the great metropolis of Shanghai itself, two years later.

As my encounter with the parading soldiers demonstrated, the communists had failed to turn the city into docility by the time the Korean War began. Shanghai had been under intense psychological pressure for more than a year, and propaganda drums began beating as soon as the North Koreans attacked. The newspapers screamed, universally and loudly, that the north had been assaulted by the South Koreans. Few Chinese in Shanghai had any way of knowing differently, but they showed little tendency to believe the charge or to concern themselves over the Koreans, who for centuries had been considered an inferior race. Neither were my students and other friends aroused, at first, by the government's attempt to inflame anti-Western nationalism over the war and over the threat of "American invasion," although nationalism is deeply ingrained within them.

The Korean conflict, in many ways, was as frustrating for political reasons to Peiping as to Washington. Americans were deeply disturbed by being told that one out of every three GIs captured by the Chinese helped the enemy in some way, and 21 out of 4,400 actually defected to communism. But the proud, face-conscious Chinese communist rulers must have been far more deeply wounded by their record. In the first foreign war of the new communist regime, 14,000 out of 22,000 captured Chinese soldiers chose to remain in the free world after the final truce.

From within China I was able to see the profound influence exerted on the undecided Chinese by the first conscious and unconscious "confessions" of captured Americans, particularly their admissions of "germ warfare." I did not believe these at the time and, like many others, I dismissed them casually. But I was seeing from the inside the effect and importance of brainwashed prisoners long before undergoing this technique myself.

Five months before there was a military need for Chinese forces in Korea, the communists began a systematic campaign to sign up "volunteers" to aid their "North Korean brothers." They did this with typical organization and typical callousness. Night after night, patriotic rallies were staged in the compound of the boys' high school, beneath my window in the seminary. All students over sixteen years of age were forced to attend by communist bullies who took charge of the meetings and sometimes seemed to run them like a kangaroo court. Speeches were loud, long and passionate and punctuated frequently by the thunder of Chinese gongs. The theme always was the same—the strength of New China, the solidarity and power of the communist nations, the "benevolent" leadership of Soviet Russia, and the need for every student to enlist in the People's Volunteer Army. I could not escape the whiplash crack of the speeches, the shattering roll of the gongs—and a searing personal sorrow.

The students themselves were deeply troubled and confused by the pressures mounting around them. The communist cadres—self-styled "progressives"—immediately signed up for military service in a frenzy of "patriotism." Every time the students walked through the gate of the compound to their classes they passed by an "honor roll" containing the names of communist "volunteers." They also walked beneath gruesome propaganda cartoons, similar to those plastered throughout the city, showing among other subjects American bombs dropping on hospitals and American soldiers stabbing small children. In the rallies, the students were subject to a mass mood, generated by the gong-backed speeches. "Patriotism" was hammered into them in almost every class, where the cadres would shoulder the professors aside and take over. The authorities permitted a few French and Chinese Fathers to continue teaching, but some lay teachers had been fired for displaying coolness toward the communist program.

Nevertheless, many students came to me and to the other priests seeking counsel. They said they did not fear American invasion and did not want to participate in a war to impose on the Korean people the communist system which they themselves opposed. Talking with innuendo and suggestion, the only prudent approach in a period filled with informers, we advised them to stand on their rights and continue their studies. Some of the young idealists were troubled by the moral problem of warfare, and these were reminded that no one should voluntarily bear arms in an unjust war.

Still, some of the noncommunist students did enlist, most of them out of apparently genuine patriotism. They were processed quickly and prepared to depart for military training. Then they discovered that all the progressives miraculously had failed their physical examinations and were rejected for military service. The authorities obviously wanted to keep their trained agents on hand to indoctrinate other students. Those who had been duped, complained so loudly and so often, however, that some of the cadres had to be sent off toward military training, to save face; although they probably ended up in some other safe assignment.

The mental torment which the noncommunist youths were undergoing was often hidden beneath prideful cheerfulness. But I saw it exposed one night when one of the most promising among them knocked softly on my door.

Wong, at nineteen, was husky and handsome, a natural

leader and an excellent student. He had been snatched from the sterile countryside by one of China's perpetual miracles and was headed toward a life of promise.

"Father, I have come to say good-by," he said, with the simple peasant directness to which he still clung. When I drew him into the room, he began to talk, softly and urgently, and I saw that he hungered to express himself freely. He had been inducted into the air force, the favored service, and was being trained as a jet pilot. The authorities had recognized his capacity but, because he was Catholic, they intensified his indoctrination. His religion was attacked particularly, for the Catholic Church had been branded as an instigator of the Korean War.

"Do you suppose," he asked, "that, after knowing you and the other Fathers, I could ever call you 'imperialist running dogs'?" He shook his head. "No, they'll never make me say that."

As he left, after many hours, he turned and said with the poetic emotion which the Chinese do not always attempt to hide: "Good-by, Father, we'll meet again in heaven."

I learned then that the cold knife of sorrow can strike anywhere, in war.

Then, in the early winter of 1950, after the Chinese had entered the combat, the controlled press began reporting the dolorous "confessions" of captured GIs. These admissions startled the city—particularly the later accounts of germ warfare—and heightened the confusion of Chinese still resisting the pressures around them. Newspapers devoted full pages to the story, reproducing the Americans' own handwriting in English, with a parallel Chinese translation. Hammering on the germ warfare theme, the papers published pictures of the alleged germ bombs, together with diagrams which purported to show how the bombs operated, and elaborate explanations of the manner in which the germs were supposed to be released, ready for infection, when they hit the ground. Pictures of rats, spiders and flies—all reported to be infected—were shown against the snow of North Korea.

This campaign was conducted with the thoroughness, persistence and fanaticism that only communists can generate. Large amounts of literature were turned out on the subject, and it became required reading in all classes everywhere— dragged into courses on current history, English, Chinese literature, biology and hygiene. It was the constant theme for the "voluntary discussion groups," by which the Chinese help brainwash themselves, held daily after school and sometimes lasting until late night.

It did not matter whether the American writing the "confession" did so because he thought no one would believe it or for some other reason. It did not matter that the United States repeatedly denied the charge from Washington and at the United Nations, where the communists brought it for further propaganda. No one questioned whether germs or infected rats and insects could survive a bomb explosion or the North Korean snows. Apparently, no one wondered why American commanders would create an epidemic in a battle area they expected to occupy.

The germ campaign was quite successful, largely because the handwritten confessions of U.S. prisoners made it appear authentic. Moreover, the Chinese, like most Asians, have an unbalanced fear of germs, which they do not understand, and their folklore is strewn with superstitions about them. Every major Asian nation, including Russia, has been accused by opponents in various wars of dropping germ bombs; and this often was the most insistent propaganda charge. During their long conflict with Japan, the Chinese Nationalists repeatedly indicted the Japanese for germ warfare and, no doubt, built up instant receptivity among their own people. Consequently, the American documents created sufficient confusion so that every rumor of sickness aroused terror and evident resentment against the United States.

Two students from the Tientsin area brought this feeling to me one afternoon. They had received a letter casually mentioning that their mother and sisters all were ill. Knowing that the mail was censored, they had come to expect casualness to hide serious news.

"Do you think there is an epidemic?" they asked. "Should we drop out of school and go home?"

We learned later, of course, that the illnesses were only colds. And the explanation was equally simple for another student who became agitated when informed, by a brief note in a letter, that his doctor-father was unusually busy.

These students were by no means friendly to communism or susceptible to it. But the steady propaganda campaign had bored into them so that they had begun to believe in germ warfare and had begun to fear any hint of illness. For the doubters, a communist cadre had only to say: "Don't believe us. Read the Americans' own words, or listen to their broadcasts on Radio Peking." From that came the automatic, often unspoken, acceptance of the concept that American planes were attacking the Chinese mainland itself, if only with germ bombs.

At the time I rejected these confessions as pure fabrications. Only six years later did I learn that the communists had no need to fabricate. They had devised a method of practical psychology which, when backed by force or its threat, was designed to weaken the victim's will, distort his principles and make him progressively more amenable to authority and control. It was under this influence that most of the confessions were made. The essentials of this type of brainwashing had been applied years before to political prisoners in Russia and Eastern Europe. The Chinese communists made it a standard tactic in their effort to enslave their own people.

Lieutenant Colonel William E. Mayer, the army psychiatrist who directly or indirectly examined more than one thousand of the American prisoners from Korea, estimated that under the influence of this technique one out of three Americans knowingly and actively collaborated with the enemy in some way at one time or another. "One out of six (almost 15 per cent)," he said, "were consistent, dedicated, hard-core collaborators with an enemy of the United States then engaged in shooting other Americans throughout the stage of captivity." * One out of ten acted as informers on their fellow prisoners. In one episode forty soldiers sat idly by while a corporal rolled two sick comrades out of their hut, into the snow and quick death. Twelve courts-martial eventually re-

---

* Taped lecture given at Lawrence Radiation Laboratory, Livermore, Calif., 1959. Virtually the same statistics were given by Mr. Hugh H. Milton II, Assistant Secretary of the Army under President Eisenhower, quoted by Eugene Kinkead, *In Every War But One* (W. W. Norton & Co., New York, 1959), p. 34.

As this book was going to press, a new evaluation of the Korean POW's was published (*March to Calumny*, Albert D. Biderman, Macmillan, New York, 1963). The author's purpose is to refute the thesis of widespread misconduct advanced by Kinkead, Mayer, and others. Murder and torture were used often enough by the communists so that those who resisted had to be heroically courageous. To classify the whole routine and atmosphere of Chinese communist imprisonment as a subtle form of torture is quite accurate. This aspect is neglected by Kinkead and Mayer. As will be explained later, brainwashing without force would be largely ineffective.

I agree with Biderman that the prisoners who compromised to some extent should not be judged harshly, except in those rare cases of grossly criminal or treasonous behavior. Only 10 of 4,000 have been *legally* convicted of collaboration (*op. cit.*, p. 37).

Without intending to assign guilt to anyone, however, the facts should be made clear. The communists did succeed in getting information from the prisoners which they used for the manipulation of others and for propaganda against the U.S., which was especially effective in Asia and in non-committed countries in general. Of the survivors, 91% admitted writing autobiographies and 39% admitted signing propaganda petitions. Even among the "resisters," 37% made "confessions" or "self-criticism" statements, and 25% signed propaganda petitions (*op. cit.*, p. 38). Considered objectively in themselves

sulted from the prison camps, out of 215 cases originally investigated to determine the justification for military action.

Direct physical torture—in the sense of incapacitating the victim—was used on less than 5 per cent of the 4,400 prisoners. Lieutenant Colonel Mayer reported that it was not a factor in the cases of army men who collaborated with the Chinese or assisted them in some way. But the threat of torture was continually present, and brutality of all types and degrees was practiced constantly. The threat of force is essential to ensure the maximum results from brainwashing, although the communists prefer to avoid using it.

These melancholy statistics created great shock and disbelief in the United States. I suspect this reaction has helped to perpetuate the feeling that brainwashing must have some superhuman characteristics or Americans would not have succumbed to it. This, of course, is untrue. The communists based their manipulation of the GIs upon weaknesses within the victims, and this continues to be primary. A Chinese document * evaluating the American prisoners, as quoted by

---

without relating them to what happened in other wars, these facts are significant. The usefulness of such statements to the communists and the harm done by them to the free world will be made clear in later chapters. The *immediate* purpose of brainwashing is to get such information and not to make communists of its victims.

To say that the successes of brainwashing have been grossly exaggerated is to underestimate the effectiveness of this weapon. The vast literature on the civilian prisoners released from communist China (most of them highly educated, intelligent, dedicated missionaries of diverse faiths and nationalities) gives abundant evidence of how devastating it can be. At the same time, to imply that virtually no one can resist it, is pure defeatism.

* Cf. Biderman, *op. cit.*, pp. 249–256. This document is actually a "reconstruction" from communist military reports and prison camp operations. The authentic document quoted by Biderman, when read with a practical knowledge of communist semantics, by no means refutes Mayer's interpretation. In his pithy summation, Mayer expresses accurately the essentials of the communists' cynical, materialistic estimate of the "capitalist man" in general. Personal experience has shown me the devastating effectiveness of this communist weapon.

Lieutenant Colonel Mayer, showed that the communists detected three basic characteristics which they attempted to exploit. They judged that Americans were materialistic and could be bought, for small favors. They believed the GIs had no sense of loyalty either to their friends or to their country. Finally, the communists believed the soldiers were ignorant of American history and traditions and knew little of world affairs.

The Chinese immediately segregated the Americans whom they considered to be leaders, about one in twenty men, and made little effort to influence them. The remainder were subjected to a calculated campaign of pressure, persuasion, argument and petty reward under the endless shadow of captivity and immediately available force. Every conceivable method was used, from daylong repetitive political lectures on the merits of communism to the use of food as both lure and punishment. The communists had a multitude of uses for the men who eventually came under their psychological control. A small number were trained to become spies in the United States. Many became active propagandists, either willingly or unknowingly, and the impact was great, not only in China but throughout the non-committed nations. Finally, cowed docility permitted the Chinese to rule their prisoners with a minimum use of their own manpower. They were not interested in recruiting communists, as they proved by treating with contempt the Americans who did defect.

The point is that the Chinese authorities made an organized, well-planned and scientific attack on their disorganized, apprehensive prisoners. This was as much a part of the war as gunfire at the front. Once captured, however, the majority of the GIs did not know that they still had to fight or what they were fighting. Neither, it might be added, did their commanders.

While the American prisoners were tamed by communist

psychological attack in the north, Chinese captives in the south kept their camps in frequent turmoil, captured and intimidated an American general and pinned down 15,000 heavily armed U.S. guards. The rate of later defections among the Chinese showed that this by no means was universal defiance. Communist cadres ruled the camps with ruthless power and drove their fellow prisoners into turmoil. But American authorities, as unprepared as the GIs for this prison camp war, were virtually helpless to weed out and segregate the communist agents.

This mutual unpreparedness appears to have been remedied, to a substantial degree, and it can be presumed that there will be no mass repetition of Korea. But the nefarious aspect of this war of wills is that each soldier—each person—is his own army and must learn for himself the use of the full range of necessary defensive weapons. Early experiences of American GIs in South Viet Nam indicate, unfortunately, that troops again may have been sent into battle without fully knowing their enemy. Korea proved, for instance, that the GI needs to be as familiar with the enemy's psychological weapons as with his own gun. Much of the propaganda which became so effective in the Korean camps was obtained by trapping the captive into cooperating when he did not realize how fully he was doing so. Furthermore, if the Americans had known the importance of the germ warfare appeal to Asian minds, it is probable they would have been more careful of their comments. It is in this respect that I hope my own experiences, when analyzed in relation to each phase of communist tactics, may be helpful.

The best-prepared front-line soldier is helpless, however, unless he also knows what he is fighting for. The origins of the sad story in Korea, as the psychologists have pointed out, go back to an uncertain heritage. The most vulnerable prisoners lacked moral convictions and a sense of their own inherent dignity. They lacked strong patriotism, in the old-fashioned sense. Without these basic elements, and others of a similar nature, the individual is defenseless against brainwashing, just as he is supine before the bully in his own block at home. I do not presume to say that my experiences can save a man with no moral strength of his own, although even then they may help him to avoid traps.

The essence of the communist attack is to separate the individual from every source of his strength as a human being. To understand this, it may be helpful to recall how Peking first used this tactic on a national scale to enslave its own people.

Chapter two

SHANGHAI
NIGHTMARE

AT THE OUTBREAK OF THE KOREAN WAR, China itself was only in the first stages of its own brainwashing. The process had barely begun in Shanghai, for the communists moved with step-by-step thoroughness and caution. In the beginning the purpose of their manipulations was not evident to most of us living in the city, and even the vast majority of Chinese were fooled. But it is clear in retrospect that, from the moment of power, the communist regime set out to brainwash the world's largest nation into obedience. This was the planned psychological murder of more than six hundred million people. The gigantic effort still continues.

On a national level, as well as in individual cases, brainwashing is designed not to create communists but to make its

27

victims act in the communist way. That means absolute obedience and dependence upon the state. All reservations, mental and physical, to the requirements or teachings of the state are to be eliminated, in the interest of unqualified obedience. Every weapon of the totalitarian regime is devoted to that end. The massive and endless internal propaganda campaign conducted by Peking, for instance, is to make the millions conform, not to convert them. In time, as the communist leader, Mao Tse-tung has said, the vacuum of soul and mind can be filled with communism, but he added that the state was willing to wait for five or ten years, or more.* Meanwhile, the power of the government is dedicated to the complete enslavement of a people known for their intractability and the fierce independence of their thinking.

In many ways Shanghai was the most difficult and the most important target in this campaign. It was the largest foreign-built city in the country, and perhaps the most Occidental in outlook. The Shanghailanders were accustomed to considerable freedom. For generations they had been shaped by a variety of foreign influences which washed into the port cities but did not always penetrate into the countryside. Except for intermittent fighting, Shanghai had escaped the major impact of the Japanese war which, from its start in 1937, remodeled the countryside and contributed to the eventual communist victory. During this conflict the communists built up a power base and tested their methods of psychological control in the areas under their guns. They had penetrated Shanghai, with subversion and propaganda, but did not dominate it. Control

---

* Cf. *Communiqué of the Tenth Plenary Session of the Eighth Central Committee,* presided over by Mao himself, *New China News Agency,* Sept. 28, 1962. ". . . throughout the historical period of proletarian revolution and proletarian dictatorship, throughout the historical period of transition from capitalism to communism—*which will last scores of years or even longer—*there is class struggle between the socialist road and the capitalist road." (Author's italics)

of the city became vital to the regime for both political and prestige reasons. Therefore, the best agents and the most effective techniques were directed toward this colossus, the landmark of rejected colonialism in China; and in many respects a benevolent landmark.

While the communists poured down the country toward them, the Shanghailanders braced themselves for the murder and pillage always associated with the innumerable revolutionary conquests in China's long history. Frenzied hopelessness dominated the city during its final days of freedom in 1948 and 1949. It goaded the people into nervous restlessness, intensifying the clamor and driving everyone, from the poverty-stricken to the incredibly wealthy, into outbursts of purposeless energy. As usual, the city's mood was reflected by the money market, the barometer of a people perpetually accustomed to instability. During the final six months of freedom, the value of the Chinese dollar dropped from a rate of 4 to 1 U.S. dollar to the incredible figure of 14 million to 1. Shopkeepers refused paper currency and demanded silver. To live, the people withdrew hoarded silver dollars from their hiding places under floor boards and inside the walls of their houses. Then began one of the most fantastic spectacles in the history of doomed cities.

On every major street corner, in those dying days of Shanghai, money-changers set up business in the middle of swirling street crowds. They operated within sight—and earshot—of our church, and I watched them often. Throughout the day the money-changers—a breed of men distinguished by the calculated impassiveness of their faces—were surrounded by clamoring, pushing throngs of Chinese. All were carrying hoards of heavy, old-fashioned Chinese silver dollars stacked alongside the inside of their arms, up to elbows and armpits, like poker chips. In this open-air gambling den, they were buying and selling U.S. dollars to get negotiable money for food and, perhaps, to make a slight profit as the city collapsed. The same scene was duplicated hundreds of times throughout the sprawling metropolis of six millon people. They conducted these shrieking, tireless transactions until the very evening when, with scattered rifle fire, the communists entered Shanghai, on May 25, 1949.

Then, everything miraculously disappeared—the money-changers, the silver dollars, the yelling crowds. The Shanghai-landers stayed at home, many of them told me, to see how their new masters would behave. But nothing happened. The city changed hands with little trouble and almost no bloodshed. Slowly the fears of my Chinese friends began to die, and the city itself relaxed. The letdown was doubly dramatic, because the ruthlessness of communism had been well advertised, sometimes by advance communist agents themselves. When this appeared to be false, the Chinese were flooded with hope; for unrealized fear has a tendency to become unwarranted optimism. While I did not share this feeling, for I had studied Marxism-Leninism closely for many years, it was difficult to convince my Chinese students and my friends that the façade might be deceptive.

This was the first move in the communist pattern of control. Leniency, in place of anticipated brutality, established a liaison and a measure of trust between the people and their new government. Communist force was constantly present and always visible, for soldiers continually roamed the streets. But the people, in general, knew only relief. After the first few days they accepted and ignored the soldiers and the increased numbers of police.

Again, the money-changers reflected the new atmosphere. The communists had brought in their own printed currency, issuing it at an official rate of about 400 to 1 U.S. dollar. It held its ground for a brief period, then the value began to inch downward until it reached the rate of 30,000 to 1. The people might trust the government more than they previously thought possible, but the sharp businessmen whose opinions influenced the money market did not respect communist ability to maintain economic stability. So, with the exchange rate falling, the money-changers began to reappear, one by one, on their familiar street corners.

As I watched one day, our neighborhood broker—a scholarly man, with a thin smoky wisp of gray beard—took his place in the usual street crowd. A few pedestrians glanced at him, at first, with cautious recognition, then hurried on. The money-changer simply stood there, in silent contemplation, with his hands folded together inside the crossed long sleeves of his blue gown. No currency was in sight, and he might have been a scholar memorizing data on the movement of shoppers. Finally, a man approached him and whispered into his ear. With swift sleight of hand, a stack of silver dollars disappeared into the gown, and the stranger stuffed greenbacks into a money belt as he walked away. A nearby policeman said nothing, but instead only looked bored—intentionally, I thought. Business picked up, and soon the transactions were conducted openly. The policeman still said nothing. As the crowd grew, a couple of soldiers in uniform joined it and watched curiously.

Before long the money-changers were back in operation at every major intersection. Soon they attracted the same clamorous throngs of precommunist days, armed with fresh supplies of heavy silver dollars and new interest in perhaps the freest form of free enterprise. The transactions continued for several weeks, on almost the same incredible scale as before. The authorities did nothing and their already controlled press remained silent on this question. This additional sign of liberality was greeted with a renewed sense of relief and relaxation. Many Chinese began to comment about the benevolence of the new regime. They seemed ready to accept it as another of the interminable Chinese governments which have swept into power over the centuries with loud gong-booming promises of change without, in fact, changing anything. Forgotten was the fact that Marxism-Leninism itself would be discredited if it had to rely upon this simple but fundamental practice of capitalism to maintain economic viability.

Then it happened. The money-changers disappeared, once more, all together, and no one could locate them. The majority ended up in jail, arrested without warning and denied communication with their families. The silver dollars also disappeared completely. The money market was closed tightly —and permanently. The communist authorities had waited until they could capture the largest number of brokers and the largest amount of silver. When they pounced, their preparations were so thorough that they eliminated the entire operation with a single effort. The state had shown its extensive power for the first time.

Rudely jolted, the people began muttering complaints, but they scarcely had time to voice them before the second step was taken in the communist control campaign. I encountered this unique maneuver one morning while riding in a pedicab in the center of the former International Settlement. The streets still were cluttered with pedestrians and with all manner of vehicles from buses to bicycles. The bustle gave an appearance of normalcy to the city, and the usual harsh cries of impatience from snarled traffic were beguilingly nonpolitical. Then my pedicab whirled past the Central Police Station, a frowning stone building which dominated the street. A new sign had been erected across its façade, demanding in large and bold Chinese characters that all "Spies Register Here." As my driver plunged deeper into the traffic, I began to chuckle. The sign first struck me as a monstrous joke, as it did many others who saw it.

llages. In
attacker.
ermore,
s a tool
e basic
social
only
ch im-
is was
tion-
inese
ugh
one
me
ese
o,
ut

g
f
s

he message quickly appeared over
plastered, in three-foot high char-
wall in the city. The press began an
, under blaring page-one headlines,
should proceed to register with the
point many Chinese still were chuck-
intended no humor by proposing that
uld surrender voluntarily. Instead, the
peal underlined the thoroughness of their
psychology.

ncient and often honorable profession in
s and warlordism had divided the country
roughout most of its history. Moreover, when
Chinese left the mainland for Formosa, many
rcover agents loyal to them remained behind.
ubt hoped to flush out these legitimate and
angerous enemies through the new campaign,
is doubtful if the authorities expected trained
trapped by this crude approach. But the attack on
a far deeper purpose. The existence of a Chinese
n power on Formosa meant that the civil war con-
and therefore the Chinese still had a mental choice
n the Nationalists and the communists. Peking used
reat of Nationalist invasion as a means of welding its
le closer together and of demanding greater sacrifices. In
atmosphere, anyone not openly and ardently in favor of
communist regime was regarded as pro-Nationalist, even
ough he might only be neutral. For the Communist Party
ank and file and those persuaded to follow them, the luke-
warm Chinese automatically became enemies of the state and
therefore spies. The anti-spy drive, then, was designed first
to arouse group pressure against those remaining aloof from
communist hysteria. Many other elements of mass psychology
were involved in this aspect of the campaign, including tradi-

tional and strong Chinese loyalties to their home v
the mass mood these had to be defended against any

The Nationalist, or Kuomintang, government, furt
was described constantly in communist propaganda
of foreign powers, particularly the United States. T
teaching of communism was that the real or expecte
gains for the downtrodden could be secured or obtain
when these foreign "imperialists" were reduced to su
potency that they could not again "enslave" China. Th
a consequential appeal to the strong and reasonable n
alism of the Chinese; an emotion which had led many Ch
to accept communism, or to avoid opposing it, even th
they were not attracted by the ideology itself. Thus an
accused of favoring the Nationalists automatically bec
accused of supporting the foreign powers against Chi
nationalism. Therefore, he was spying for the foreigners w
in propaganda, only were using the Nationalists to carry
their imperialist scheme to recapture mainland China.

But the communists portrayed themselves as regardir
these spies not with venom but with the sad benevolence
a disappointed parent. There was no need for fear, the pres
screamed, because the People's government knew that the
spies were victims of foreign propaganda. They had only to
register, confess their sins and be rejuvenated by "reeducation." Then they could return to their homes and families to
begin life again under the New Republic. If this noble offer
was ignored by the guilty, the regime would locate them any-
way, for it already had accumulated all the necessary information about their activities. In that case, the implication was,
the spies would be punished severely.

Finally, the press began to emphasize the need for speed
in purging all spies from society, for only then could work
proceed on building the new state. Therefore, anyone with
knowledge of spies should volunteer information about them

to the authorities, thereby rendering a meritorious service to the state. Gradually, on this basis, the regime built up a step-by-step campaign to persuade or frighten the Chinese into betraying each other. In every school, every factory, every office meetings were called almost daily for periods of "self-criticism." In these meetings, under group pressure and the effect of propaganda, each individual was required to confess and renounce his sins publicly before the group. In time, he was led to condemn the "false" activities of others. Eventually, betrayal became a method of behavior, and many condemned those they knew for fear that they themselves would be condemned first. So, children were taught to betray their parents; and the parents their children. Friends, as well as enemies, denounced each other. Some, believing in the benevolence of the regime, thought perhaps they were helping to save a loved one. Others acted from venom or verbal hypnosis. Fundamentally, however, the self-criticism groups worked on the deep and fundamental Chinese dread of losing face before his acquaintances; a built-in concept aiding in group conformity.

Peking's purpose, of course, was to use the people to uncover opponents or actual enemies of the state. The communists had employed the same basic technique earlier, in the rural regions of the north, to goad the peasants into demanding land from their landlords. The state then "benevolently" took the land, in response to this appearance of the popular wish, and went through the motions of delivering it to the peasants. Soon, however, the state robbed the farmers of the same land through a series of subterfuges, beginning with the so-called "cooperative" farm system.

Both in the countryside and in the city, these campaigns to arouse the people into doing the state's work constituted brainwashing. The various appeals and pressures were designed to create a mass mood for the performance of a specific act on behalf of the regime. It did not matter whether the participants were communists or whether any large percentage of them actually believed they were doing right. The essence of brainwashing is to make a man perform an act desired by the communists, even though at the time and later he may realize that it is wrong. His will to heed his conscience has been so weakened by the numerous influences directed against him that he has no strength to resist communist demands. Then, when the communists need the individual or the group to perform another service, brainwashing is revived and the process repeated. In this sense the immediate aim of psychological attack is to move one step at a time. Its full impact is directed toward the creation of what may be only a temporary mood during the performance of the desired action. Once brainwashed, however, the individual or the group becomes progressively more susceptible to control for the subsequent acts desired by the communists.

In Shanghai the communists achieved only limited success through the use of persuasion, propaganda and group pressures. A few Chinese felt, perhaps, that they might benefit by conformity, but the majority held back, remembering the sudden disappearance of the money-changeres and their silver. So the final and necessary ingredient of brainwashing—force—was introduced. The press threatened harsh punishment for any spies who failed to register and, particularly, for anyone who knew about spy activities and failed to report them. This threat worked, to some extent, but not completely. Life continued with remarkable surface normalcy. Businesses were open, and the city continued to function. Travel was constant to the outside world, particularly Hong Kong, and the authorities at first did not interfere with it. Despite the shadow of force and the uncertainty of the first twenty-three months under communist control, Shanghailanders did not flee in any large numbers when they had the chance. Many made several trips outside the country, always returning to their homes in Shanghai with apparent confidence that the regime did not intend to go beyond the group pressures it had used up to that time. For the communists, however, gentle persuasion clearly was insufficient to ensure control over the city.

Then, in one swift strike, twenty thousand people were rounded up and thrown into prison on the night of April 27, 1951. They had been shadowed for weeks by thousands of special government agents and military and regular police.* The files of the New People's Republic were crammed with information. The arrests were announced in a virulent press campaign which hammered incessantly on the "crimes" of these "enemies of the state." The crimes were detailed— possession of short-wave radio sets; membership in the Kuomintang Party of the Nationalists; expressed hostility to the communists, even before they won control of the city, and so on endlessly. Many of the captives were accused of actual espionage, through a network allegedly operated from Hong Kong, and these were to be "liquidated," the press cried.

As the press campaign continued, it was apparent that the people were being brainwashed into expecting and demanding mass trials for the culprits. Mounting hysteria made it unwise for foreigners to travel about the city, and we remained most of the time within our island, in the compound at Zikawei. But the tumult came directly to us through our students and the friends still willing to visit us. Indeed, we could not evade it, because the noise of street mobs and the screech of loudspeakers and, finally, the constant din of continual radio broadcasts became a standard part of life, and

---

* Incredible as these statistics seem, in a later, less violent purge the communists themselves reported that they used the following personnel: 750,000 full-time investigators, 1 million activists, 3,280,000 part-time investigators. These figures do not include the regular army and security police, who also play an active role in such crackdowns. cf. Report on the *Su Fan Movement* in *Hsueh Hsi* (*Study*), Peking, Jan. 3, 1958.

isolation was impossible.

The People's Trials were held at the Shanghai Race Course, once a green oasis built by the foreign "colonialists" in the center of the International Settlement. Large enough to accommodate a nine-hole golf course, the race course compound was the only open space in a jammed section of the modern city. Tall and graceful hotels and office buildings peered over the track, and the jumbled disarray of Chinees slums crowded against its outside walls.

Huge crowds were persuaded or forced to attend, because the effect of the People's Trials depended upon the maximum participation of the "people." Jammed into the grandstand and spread across the grass of the infield, tens of thousands surrounded a makeshift stage in the center of this open-air courtroom at the start of each day's proceedings. The accused stood, lonesome, at center stage while a parade of "witnesses" denounced their crimes with an alarming mixture of half-truths and distorted facts. Their high-pitched denunciations raked the crowds through loudspeakers and snarled throughout the city by radio. All work and study stopped, while everyone in schools, factories and office buildings gathered in special assemblies to listen respectfully to the "voice of the people." As the accusations grew more shrill, my Chinese friends told me, communist cadres circulated through the trial crowds, watching the reaction of the spectators and by their presence warning them to respond properly. Then, at the proper moment, the crowd would be asked its opinion. With the communist agents leading, the invariable hysterical response roared from thousands of throats was: "He is guilty!" "He is a counterrevolutionary!" "Kill him!" A bullet in the back of the head quickly ended each case.

To be sure that the full impact of these executions reached the greatest possible mass of the population, many of the condemned criminals would be paraded throughout the city in open-back trucks decorated with huge banners proclaiming that "unreformable counterrevolutionaries must die." Crowds would be "invited" to Kiang Wan Airfield in a northern suburb of the city to witness how efficiently and economically the new regime dispatched those who opposed it. Soon the expression "going to Kiang Wan" became a melancholy synonym for death.

In this Roman circus atmosphere the state once more "benevolently" responded to the wishes of the people by killing its enemies. By this use of brainwashing the communists eliminated their most obvious opponents—thousands of them—in the country's largest city.

The trials established the terror base for communist power, which continues today. The masses quickly learned that, as Mao Tse-tung later said, the "new democracy" meant that the Party alone had the right to designate who is a "person," that is, a citizen of the state, and who is an "enemy." *

In quick succession, the state launched the remainder of its first nationwide campaigns to prune China down to communist size. At the end of 1951 it opened an extensive drive against "corruption, waste and bureaucratism," the beginning of the San Fan or Three-Anti movement. While this marked the start of the organized effort to eliminate all private business, the campaign permitted the government to remove its own deadwood and to convince the masses that self-purge showed its sincerity. The momentum of the Three-Antis lasted for several months. Then, after a short lull, it merged with a far more extensive purge, the Wu Fan or Five-Anti movement. It was designed to remove "five evils" which were so loosely defined and applied that the entire industrial

---

* Cf. "On the Correct Handling of Contradictions Among the People," Speech by Mao Tse-tung on Feb. 27, 1957, published with revisions (probably by Mao himself) by New China News Agency, June 18, 1957. In his *Democratic Dictatorship* (1949) Mao expounds the same theory, which was applied as early as 1927 and again in 1942.

and merchant class was covered, as were all opponents the regime had failed to eliminate through previous efforts. The advertised purpose was to eliminate "bribery, tax evasion, fraud, theft of state secrets, and leakage of state economic secrets."

Actually, the Five-Anti drive was designed to undermine capitalism, and it hit Shanghai heavily. Instead of the swift vengeance of the anti-spy movement, however, the communists moved in this instance with the deliberate attempt to erode opposition. They spread the arrest of prime suspects over a period of six months, instead of one night. Prisoners were fined heavily, but imprisoned in most cases for only a few months, rather than years. Then they were released, to spread among their friends horrified tales of conditions in jail and, perhaps most of all, to describe the appalling helplessness felt by proud men reduced to dependence upon the whim of their jailers. The communists infected the masses with the constantly reiterated theme that anyone making a profit was exploiting the people.

Despair spread quickly through once-ebullient Shanghai; the despair created by the disappearance of friends, the prolonged agony of each slow investigation, the weight of increasing uncertainty. Each of the innumerable trials usually involved crushing fines, as high as 10,000 U.S. dollars. In many cases this amount absorbed all savings, and the pressure of public opposition reduced business to profitlessness. The communist goal was clear—to reduce this powerful opposition class to supine dependence upon the state. In this battle for men's souls, the proud, reckless, gambler's spirit of Shanghai finally broke. Businessmen jumped from the city's buildings toward death in such numbers that the communists had to post antisuicide guards atop the tallest structures. Until then, hurtling bodies became a menace to pedestrians on downtown streets. Every hospital was filled, even to crowded corridors, by broken men and women who had attempted suicide or who had been struck by falling bodies.

The communists maintained this corrosive pressure against businessmen for four years. None was permitted to quit operations but all were required to maintain production or continue in business despite the squeeze of official and public opposition and rising labor demands. Finally, Peking achieved its goal. The businessmen themselves begged the state to take over their enterprises, and once more a "beneficent" regime complied when full-fledged socialism was installed in January, 1956. I was taken out of jail one night to see for myself the people dancing in the streets with joy "to respectfully thank the government" for confiscating their businesses.

Meanwhile, other aspects of these campaigns clawed at the fabric of Chinese society. All private schools were taken over and linked with the curricula of public institutions, so that the communist "truth" could be taught at the earliest possible moment. The teachings of Confucius, which had served as China's conscience for centuries, were belittled and repudiated. The cherished family system, which had held the individualistic Chinese together, was attacked bitterly and weakened. In short, the communists undertook the gigantic task of creating a society which in major respects was almost the complete reverse of the traditional life the Chinese built for themselves when they had the choice. A people who loved laughter and moments of wildness and who gambled continually and almost by instinct were told to live within humorless puritanical restraints. If, at the same time, the communists introduced hygiene and reduced corruption, they provided no substitute for the elements of Chinese character, common to all races and regions, which they attempted to eliminate.

Peking succeeded in this disjointed transformation through more than the mere use of raw force. In each of these major campaigns the people themselves were brainwashed into carrying out the state's wishes, even when the purpose was to amputate characteristics to which the majority instinctively sought to cling. Similarly, brainwashing was the decisive element in prodding China into the feverish race for modernity during the "great leap forward," complete with backyard steel furnaces. It was the driving factor behind the creation of the infamous commune system in farms and factories, at the final sacrifice of Chinese independence and love of family. These latter two campaigns failed for a variety of reasons, including their inapplicability to China or, perhaps, to any country. The point, however, is that the people were driven into them by the use of mass psychology, even though at the time many thousands, no doubt, consciously recognized that they were helping to destroy what they really wanted to retain. If, instead, brainwashing had turned them into devout communists, there would have been no clash of conscience. And there would have been none of the psychological reaction among the farmers which helped wreck the commune program, after the effects of brainwashing wore off.

This psychological attack is designed only as a mass weapon. The communists may use it to force the people into destroying their enemies, but they waste little time in a direct attempt to brainwash their identifiable opponents. They know it will not work against resolute resistance. In these cases, they rely upon the surer methods of murder and indefinite imprisonment. Peking itself has admitted killing ten million persons in the name of communism. The real figure, as given to me by Chinese in a position to know, probably totals around twenty million.* It is a closely guarded secret how many millions are living under the various stages of captivity decreed by the state for political prisoners. This includes vast

---

* Richard L. Walker, *China Under Communism* (Yale University Press, New Haven, 1955), all of Chap. 9, especially pp. 219–222. *Time,* March 5, 1956: 20 million "disposed of," 23 million in slave labor battalions.

slave labor establishments, often maintained on the inhospitable and undeveloped edges of the country, where recalcitrants are sent for "reform through labor." Again, the purpose is not to turn them into communists but to use their muscles and, in doing so, to brainwash them into sufficient obedience so that a minimum of surveillance is necessary.

In all, then, a substantial part of the total population of the original communist state has proved to be intractable to brainwashing or has been considered so by the shrewd practicing psychologists who administer the technique. The percentage becomes higher by eliminating the remote tribes and villages which, while included in the nation's population estimates, remain outside the main stream of communist action.

As this outline of Shanghai's story shows, the communists moved against their own people with circumspection and subterfuge. Many thousands were trapped before they realized what was happening to them or before they discerned the full extent of the control tactics being employed. If they had been forewarned, the resistance rate unquestionably would have been higher. The Chinese found that, once trapped, capitulation in subsequent instances became progressively easier and resistance progressively more difficult.

This point was proved, on a small scale, by our own students. Before the state took over our schools we tried our best to prepare the young Chinese for the ordeals we knew were ahead of them. Teachers and professors had laid the groundwork by instilling the scholastic respect for truth so revered by the naturally philosophical minds of the Chinese. The instructors had thoroughly taught the principles of freedom through its long development in Europe and the United States and had attempted to create an irreversible respect for it. The communists, of course, attacked this concept by every possible means. So, until we were finally removed from all contact with the students, we conducted a running fight with the communists for the minds and souls of these young Chinese.

The communists, in endless lectures and public "discussion groups," preached class hatred and class warfare. When puzzled students came surreptitiously to us, we taught brotherly love and the social ideal of mutual respect and cooperation among all classes of human beings. The communists taught absolute obedience to the state, regardless of its effects upon personal and family relationships or the human sorrow involved. Over and over we stressed the spiritual ideals of the true Chinese culture: fidelity to self, filial piety, mutual respect. The communists taught that man is only a highly developed animal. We taught human dignity. We never meddled in politics, nor did we try to incite rebellion or physical violence.

For two years the students were under relentless attack, and some were jailed. In prison they were questioned sharply, lectured on the "errors of their ways," then released. After that they were expected to cooperate. But we soon heard of an incident involving some of our own students which disproved the communist expectations.

In March, 1953, a group of youths was required to attend a large memorial service for Stalin, after the Russian dictator's death. At the door they were issued black armbands. Our students took them, with polite thanks, then used the armbands to wipe the dust from their shoes. They were rebuked strongly for not showing the proper reverence for the communist leader and were forced to apologize publicly in a subsequent self-criticism group. "Yes," these students admitted, "we behaved badly during this period of mourning. But we beg that our behavior be excused, because this is the first chance we have had to mourn a great communist leader. We promise to do much better when the next one dies." They left little doubt they were referring to Mao Tse-tung. We had

44

never advocated such open defiance, but word of the students'
gesture gave us the warming reassurance that our teachings
had been neither forgotten nor submerged beneath communist doctrine.

The students also demonstrated their defiance in another
way during those early days of uncertainty and travail. The
constant threat of imprisonment was so strong that many of
them kept at hand a small bundle of their personal necessities
wrapped in a large cloth. One day when summoned for questioning, several entered the headquarters of the Security Police carrying these bundles.

"What are those for?" the police asked.

"We've brought our clothes," the students replied. "We're
tired of running back and forth between headquarters and
school. So lock us up now and get it over with. We're not
going to renounce our beliefs."

Such boldness baffled the communists. Their greatest fear
was of being mocked. If psychological persuasion did not
work, their only recourse was to physical force. But the previously determined time for the application of force had not
been reached when this incident occurred. So the authorities
could only look into those determined young faces, with the
thinly veiled mockery in their eyes, and admit defeat. None
of the youths was punished on that occasion, despite the grave-
ness of the offense to communist minds. When force finally
became standard in 1955, many went off to jail rather than
sacrifice their self-respect. Seven years later, under incredible
hardships and pressure, they were still true to their honor
(trust).

The Chinese communists never trusted their intellectuals.
They have been consistently more concerned with domi-
nating scholars, scientists and students than in utilizing their
talents for the welfare of a nation crying for talent. Consequently, the ultimate development of brainwashing tactics

against these elements appeared to follow a logical progression of force which could not have been prevented, except in the unlikely event that total capitulation removed all suspicion from the suspicious communist authorities. First, the seniors of all high schools and colleges were required, as a prerequisite to graduation, "voluntarily" to pledge "mobilization" for the good of the fatherland. For those continuing their education, this meant that the state henceforth would determine the schools they would attend, the courses of study they would be permitted, and ultimately the work they would be allowed to do. Those leaving school were equally dependent upon the state for the nature and location of their employment and the rate of advancement—for the rest of their lives. Needless to say, these matters were decided by the Party, which judged each person primarily for his political "reliability." Second, the degree of psychological brainwashing directed against the students was intensified after the first two years. While I was able to watch our students I saw that many resented and resisted the impact of mass rallies, self-criticism meetings and the disciplinary controls exercised by communist agents planted among them with authority to report any suspicions to the police. Since the state provided all students with board and room, only those with independent means could afford to leave school, for they could not find any employment. A few were able to do this, but the majority had to remain in their tightly controlled educational environment. Finally, the authorities attempted to break the intellectuals by sending thousands of them to labor camps, where their minds were expected to atrophy.

I have thought often of this relentless, calculated campaign against the youths I had come to love and respect, and I could not avoid contrasting their lives with my own. My high school years were during the depression, from 1931 to 1935. My father always had a position as an accountant for the

Luckenbach Steamship Co., but as times grew harder, his salary was cut, until it was only 50 or 60 per cent of the usual amount. But we did not starve, and we even were able to maintain an old Chevrolet. About one or two days before every payday we were definitely broke.

Still, we were happy. We would take the car, buy a gallon of gas, which then cost 20 cents, and drive to Ingleside Beach, near San Francisco. For another 10 cents we could buy a jumbo bag of popcorn. Then, munching the popcorn, we would sit in the car, watching the breakers crash on the shore. This was our night out, a family night for the four of us, and we enjoyed it as much as any expensive night club.

Those lean years drew us together, and all of us learned to enjoy the simple things of life. My dad was a successful man, and he and my mother shared true contentment and happiness; although most of the time they had very little money.

Many of the Chinese students were short of funds, too, and I hoped this experience would give them the same strength which had come to me. But I had one thing they could not enjoy. I had freedom to decide my fate.

During my sophomore and junior years in high school I struggled with the decision of whether to become a priest. I had been an altar boy since the age of ten and, like many other boys, I had determined then to enter the priesthood. But the final decision was harder to reach, and in those school years I began to understand the responsibility, as well as the privilege, accompanying individual freedom.

Often the thought of being separated from the warm life of our family was enough to put the idea of the priesthood out of my mind. And, despite the times, I was having a great deal of fun in school. I did not have to make too great an effort to keep up with my classes. I was able to play football, was able to swim and to participate in debating and school politics. In my senior year I was secretary of the student body and also a class officer.

Nevertheless, the urge for the priesthood was strong, and at the end of my senior year I had told my parents that I wanted to go to the seminary. They offered no objections, only wise counsel. "If you want to begin training," my dad said, "and are sure you want to, don't quit—go all the way."

This was a frightening decision for a seventeen-year-old. I realized that it rested solely with me, and that for the first time I was completely on my own. My parents and a very wise priest adviser gave me encouragement but made no attempt to influence my decision. In my desire to be absolutely sure, I postponed final judgment on the question and enrolled in the prelegal course at the University of San Francisco.

In my freshman year at college, during 1935–36, I was elected class president, but my schedule eliminated football and debating, my two prime extracurricular interests in high school. I managed to squeeze in one season of Rugby, taking perhaps undue pride from the fact that I played in the scrub as a 160-pound freshman, alongside the 220-pound varsity tackles.

Times were improving somewhat after the worst of the depression, but prices still were low enough for a college student to attain comparative affluence. I worked in the public library seven hours daily, six days a week, for an average of $45 monthly. This enabled me to pay all school expenses, buy my own clothes, help with expenses at home and retain a fair amount of spending money.

My social life blossomed accordingly, and I began to enjoy a round of student dances and parties.

The more enjoyable these occasions became, paradoxically, the more I began thinking again more strongly about the priesthood. Many nights I would come home late from an especially entertaining party, then sit by myself in the living

48

room, smoking and meditating. In those moments of deeply personal introspection, my social life seemed empty, and I began to realize that I wanted something deeper and more satisfying. I went to Mass nearly every morning, praying for guidance, and resolution slowly formed in my mind.

Finally, in the fall of 1937, I decided to be a Jesuit. I went to nearby Los Gatos, California, to begin the long training for my vocation. My preparation would end on June 4, 1953 —eleven days before I went to jail in Shanghai. Almost from the start I developed the unchanging desire to serve in China; the result of the Chinese lure in San Francisco, and the stories I had read in high school of the great Jesuit missionaries to Cathay in the sixteenth and seventeenth centuries.

Why did I finally become a priest? Primarily because of my intense gratitude to God for my own happy family life and for the ideals of the United States, which made this possible. I wanted, most sincerely, to do as much as I could to help others find the same joy and satisfaction in life, in repayment for my own blessings.

So when the communist blight settled over Shanghai and over my students, I felt the impact with double force. I never knew, of course, how much of my deep feelings I was able to transmit to the Chinese or how long they lasted.

In face of Peking's unchallenged power, it might appear that our teachings at Zikawei could have little influence or permanence. But I have been forever thankful that we gave those Chinese students what courage we could and the vision of freedom that was possible, for I am sure that those who held out longest against the authorities have been able to draw from this instruction strength to ease the rigors of their present life.

One of the most nefarious aspects of brainwashing is that the man who capitulates to it against his conscious will and therefore performs actions against his conscience is harried

49

perpetually afterward by a deepening guilt complex. This, in turn, prompts him to collaborate more easily the second time, even though the result may be equally repugnant to his conscious mind; and so self-hatred grows. Most of our students were spared this, at least.

The pressures of intellectual discontent apparently were partly responsible for Mao's campaign, in 1957, to "let a hundred flowers bloom and a hundred thoughts contend." The purpose in this move, it soon became clear, was to expose malcontents, so that the state could eliminate them, as it did in the anti-spy campaign of 1951. Before this happened, however, the "flowers" movement revealed particular unrest in all the country's main colleges. By speeches and posters stuck to campus walls, students everywhere showed they had not forgotten the fundamental human rights we tried to teach our youths nor had they ceased to hunger for them. I have wondered many times whether this feeling would have been anywhere nearly so strong in 1957 or would have existed at all if there had been no defiance from the first student victims of communism.

Far from being invincible, then, brainwashing has many significant weaknesses. It is so fundamental to Chinese communist control techniques, moreover, that each defeat, however temporary, spreads outward in distance and time like the enlarging ripples of a disturbed lake. Each victory for this tactic has the same effect. Therefore, every individual involved in brainwashing becomes important, and his importance increases in direct proportion to his exploitable value—up to captured Americans.

Most of the victims have the fundamental capacity to resist and to create an adverse chain reaction. But few, even among the Chinese, were able to use this capacity effectively until they learned, or were told, how to resist.

Brainwashing is a complex science, developed by the communists through years of intense experimentation upon human guinea pigs. In Chinese hands, it is the heart of the world's most extensive control system, and the backbone of Chinese communism itself.

Chapter three

BRAINWASHING
AS A SCIENCE

B RAINWASHING IS SO VITAL TO COMMUNIST discipline that the communists use it continually on themselves. Periodic instances of confession and self-criticism, from the Kremlin to the lowest party cell, have been widely publicized. Less attention has been given to the thousands of other brainwashing sessions which, particularly in China, absorb a considerable proportion of the time and energy of millions of people. Although the resultant economic loss is great, the communists do not regard this process as waste. Discipline is the prime Party concern, and its leaders have found that absolute obedience depends upon constantly re-invigorated psychological control. Conflicting thoughts must be eliminated repeatedly, even from converted minds. The communists justify this circumstance by the thesis that "contradictions" are inevitable and must be eradicated by Party action.

If loyal communists must be brainwashed periodically into obedience, stronger pressures obviously are necessary to produce equal docility among those with no ideological ties to the movement. The Chinese communists have developed brainwashing into a scientific technique to produce this result among masses of unreceptive people and individuals. It is a clever combination of practical psychology, of communist philosophy and of force, both psychological and physical.

On a national scale, Peking depends upon group influences and such powerful motivations as patriotism to enlarge the disciplinary controls of brainwashing. But these group instincts are dominated by fear and fear has been made into a pattern of life by thousands of police and by gigantic mobilized armies. In the brainwashing of captured American prisoners, the communists relied upon both group influence and individual pressures, again bulwarked by force. Psychological control is most intensive and most effective, however, when applied against a single prisoner, who is cut off from the influence as well as the comfort of the group. The Chinese prefer a solitary victim, as they demonstrated by seeking to destroy group solidarity among the American prisoners. Here, again, force is the indispensable factor; whether displayed by the physical act of imprisoning the victim or by the actual or threatened use of torture. Without force, brainwashing would be largely ineffective.

At the outset, then, this psychological process is far more complex and diabolical than is implied in the terms "reeducation" and "thought reform," often used by Peking. The implication of these phrases, which have been repeated by some American commentators, is that the communists merely want to convert the individual on an intellectual level. He is, presumably, to be persuaded into abandoning his alle-

53

giance for democracy and free enterprise in order to accept communism and the "people's dictatorship." This would turn brainwashing into a battle of wits, with the outcome dependent upon the prisoner's preparation to withstand the impact of propaganda and "Marxist logic." Theoretically, he can escape involvement simply by refusing to believe or by marshaling more impressive arguments. In the end he might even convert his captors. The communists themselves exploded this comforting vision of their technique by treating with the utmost contempt the American prisoners who accepted their philosophy in the Korean prison camps. Moreover if they only wanted to "sell" a superior philosophy, and believed they could do so, they would abandon force completely; for they have found that it creates strong resistance against them.

As a disciplinary measure, however, brainwashing relies upon a delicate balance of force and psychological manipulation to produce complete surrender and obedience. Whether or not the groups or individuals being used turn toward communism is secondary, at the moment, for the main purpose is to enforce control. When brainwashing is used against an individual prisoner, the question of ideology is even more remote. His arrest and imprisonment imply, to communist minds, that he is guilty of active anticommunism and, therefore, is beyond immediate conversion. It is this area of man-to-man confrontation with brainwashing that I intend to explore. Any study of the Chinese technique must begin, it seems to me, with the struggle between one man and his captors. Everyone seeking to resist brainwashing is, by necessity, forced back to dependence upon himself. In some instances, he must even willfully cut himself off from any group of which he might be a physical part.

The Chinese communists have only one purpose in brainwashing the individual. They want to turn him into a helpless instrument for any manipulation they desire. This means breaking his will so completely that obedience is absolute in every circumstance, and the will cannot reassert itself, not with even a flicker of defiance. The first step in this process is to hammer from the victim's mind all his old beliefs and convictions, all his warming memories—everything, in short, that sustains him as a human being. When this has been done, the mind becomes a vacuum and the will is deprived of the thoughts and ideals and experiences which give it strength.

This is precisely what the communists mean by their crude, but expressive, phrase "hsi-nao," literally to "wash the brain." A second phrase describing this process has equal meaning for the Chinese, although it is more difficult to translate. "Se hsiang kao t'ung" means "thought made clear," in the sense of blasting away a roadblock or some other obstruction, or totally eliminating past mental convictions. Communist authorities have shown some sensitivity to the connotations given brainwashing in the West, but they have not denied the practice. As late as 1961, its purpose was confirmed directly by Hsieh Chueh-tsai, president of Red China's Supreme Court. While defending the communist penal system against outside criticism, Hsieh noted that "imperialists disparage us by speaking of brainwashing." Instead of refuting the charge, however, he added: "Is it not excellent that the dirty things in the brain should be washed away and salutary things inserted; to reform reactionary thoughts and to accept progressive thoughts, is it not a good thing?" * Hsieh, of course, was speaking of the Chinese. For obvious reasons, he could not admit that the authorities, in most instances, had no desire to spend the time and effort required to infuse new thoughts into the mental vacuums they attempted to create.

The destruction of all the thoughts and concepts held by

* Peking *Daily Worker,* May 30, 1961.

each individual prisoner when thrown into jail is, of course, an involved and ambitious project. It cannot be done solely through propaganda or argument or even the use of force. Neither can it be achieved by prolonged imprisonment. The men who practice brainwashing—the communist officials in jails and prison camps—know this and have devised alternative methods. They are skilled practical psychologists, whatever their formal training. In their own crude, bullying way they operate like psychiatrists—but psychiatrists in reverse.

The normal psychological treatment for a disturbed patient is to relieve or eliminate the tensions which, among other causes, are created by anxiety or guilt. The communist treatment for a normal person is the attempt to create anxiety and guilt in order to produce tensions capable of driving him to a breaking point. In other words, I am convinced the communists consciously try to create in their victims a quasi-neurotic anxiety complex. The anxieties, not communist logic, are expected to blur old convictions and weaken the will into capitulation. The intent is to make the prisoner completely dependent upon his captors and, therefore, entirely submissive to them.

From the beginning of imprisonment the prisoner comes under intensive pressure designed to strip from him all the qualities and attributes of humanism. He is forced to live like an animal, he is fed like an animal, he is treated like an animal. He is required to remain silent and inactive in his cage, with no mental stimulus except that which he can create within himself. His jailers, operating under their self-made laws, have absolute control over his well-being and the extent of his servitude.

A long list of petty regulations outlaws nearly every normal human action, bringing swift punishment or threat from alert guards. In this environment minutiae soon assume major importance—a ray of sunshine, enough edible food, a bath, even the use of a lavatory. The thoughts and ideals that sustain men frequently drift into the shadows of the mind and, unless consciously revived, often are buried beneath the grimy reality of day-to-day existence.

In hopeless apathy and physical bestiality, the prisoner is expected by his captors to degenerate into a creature of instinct. The powerful motivations of fear and survival come to the surface, and such normal restraints as honor can easily become abstract and weak. The communist "psychiatrists" play upon these basic instincts while relentlessly probing each man for weaknesses to exploit. Selfishness, cruelty, greed, cupidity, subservience, self-doubt, irresolution, even an overpowering love of family—all these are tools for the communists when exposed and distorted. The Chinese decided, for instance, that their GI prisoners in Korea could be bought cheaply and lacked strong loyalties; so bits of food and threats of brutality were used regularly, and interchangeably, to produce informers and part-time collaborators. Propaganda lectures were endless, to create and enlarge doubts about the American purposes in Korea and the individual's role in that war; for the Chinese had decided their prisoners lacked sufficient knowledge of the world to refute communist arguments.

In its ultimate stage Chinese brainwashing clearly is designed to reduce its victims to absolute instinct, with painless survival the only clear reason for existence. The weak and the irresolute will try to soften their fate by ingratiation, as they have done throughout the history of wars and prisons. This might be called a quasi-psychotic state induced by the environment and by harsh reality. But this explanation is insufficient to describe the reasons for such a high percentage of instinctive behavior among the prisoners of the Chinese communists; particularly the large number of men who recognized the repulsiveness of their actions even while committing them. Consequently, I believe one significant step in the Chinese technique is the attempt to create conditioned behavior through methods now called "Pavlovism," even though some American authorities disagree.

More than fifty years ago the Russian scientist Ivan Pavlov discovered that dogs could be made to respond predictably and in the same way to signals which they had come to associate with food or with pain. By ringing the food bell he could cause the animals to salivate in anticipation. The signal for pain prompted them to withdraw.

These were called "conditioned reflexes," and subsequent experiments by other scientists have confirmed that they can be created at will among laboratory animals. Furthermore, Pavlov demonstrated that he could produce hopeless confusion among his dogs by mixing the signals, and eventually could induce a form of psychosis or mental breakdown. This discovery also has been confirmed. The point has been established that debilitating confusion is possible merely by offering or withdrawing food, but that a mixture of reward and pain produces swifter and more intensive results. Pavlov has been made into a hero in Red China and Soviet Russia, and the communists have attempted to apply his methods against human beings on many levels. These efforts involving the modern techniques of producing conditioned reflexes are termed "Pavlovism" in this study.

The identifiable use of this technique is evident in all stages of brainwashing. The offer of reward, for instance, is common in even the crudest prison, while, at the other extreme, force remains constant. The authorities continually use threat and promise as alternate approaches, then seek to mix them so completely that the prisoner eventually does not know which to expect.

The communists leave little doubt that they expect to reduce their prisoners to quasi-psychotic instinctive behavior, and then to rule them by the snap of a finger through conditioned reflexes. Instead of withdrawing a paw from pain, the human prisoner is expected to use the remainder of his intellect to buy relief by fawning on his captors or by selling out his friends or his country. In these circumstances, a confession or a piece of propaganda or a report on fellow prisoners often becomes the equivalent of the tail-wagging crawl of a mistreated dog. The communists obviously consider these acts in this way. Like the dog, moreover, the prisoner who has once capitulated never reforms his master, he only invites more mistreatment. The communists turn again and again to those who have crawled to them, because subservience has become useful once more, but they do not bother to hide their scorn for the men they misuse.

I have seen men broken by this pressure, and I have seen others so changed by it that a guard's single barked command could twist them into trembling impotence. Still others, their brains half "washed," were too reduced to instinct to resist the collaboration demanded by their captors, yet they retained enough conscious reason to know at the time that they were doing wrong. In some ways these men were the most pathetic, for self-recrimination became a new torture for them. Some men, too, have resisted the most virulent forms of brainwashing, but only after fighting every step of the way.

The communists, of course, are not the first conquerors to rule by dehumanization. They are the first, however, to develop a scientific process to produce this result. And they are the first to exalt contempt for humanity into a basic tenet of their philosophy. Brainwashing is far more than a mere technique for controlling actual prisoners. It represents communist dialectics in the purest and most intensive form. To understand the depth of this cynicism, it might be helpful to review briefly Marxism-Leninism—that is, dialectical and historical materialism—as applied to brainwashing.*

Materialism to the communists means that all reality, man included, is nothing but matter.† This material universe is governed by absolutely unchangeable and irresistible laws of evolution. The world has evolved through dialectics, or the struggle between opposing forces. Applying this dialectical struggle to human affairs, we can interpret the whole course of history and even can predict its future. The inflexible laws of nature inexorably are moving human society toward pure communism. Only those who understand these objective laws are scientific. Hence, in politics, economics, sociology and philosophy, the word "science" means communism.

The laws of human history, in this view, are determined so absolutely that, theoretically, the evolution of the world into a classless society of equals would come about even if there were no communist agitators. However, it is the "sacred duty" of those who understand this new science to speed up the process by their agitation. The communist's blind faith in this science explains his inflexibility and unchangeableness. It also explains the arrogant complacency and confidence of the dedicated communist. Referring to the communist expansion in Russia, Eastern Europe, China, and Southeast Asia—which had been foretold by Lenin—communist theorists then conclude:

> Crucial developments in the first half of this century thus provide irrefutable proof that the Communists, armed with the Marxist theory, correctly predicted the general course of history. The truth of

* *Fundamentals of Marxism-Leninism,* edited by Clemens Dutt (Foreign Languages Publishing House, Moscow, 1960), Parts I & II, *passim.*

† One should not be misled by double-talk about "mind," "spirit," "consciousness." A careful analysis of pertinent passages shows that communists are gross materialists, even though dialectical materialism is a new dynamic type.

the Marxist-Leninist conception of history has been fully borne out in practice.*

For the communists, dialectical historical materialism is a guide to action. This theory provides a scientific basis for revolutionary policy. They believe that this basic concept of history can never change and that it is not in the power of man to change it.

The communists tell us that history does not conform to man's wishes if his wishes are not in accordance with the laws of history, which are absolute and determined. They do concede that a sober, scientific analysis of objective situations and the objective course of evolution is a basis for defining the political line of the Party at the moment. As Marx said: "We must take things as they are, that is, uphold the revolutionary cause in a form that corresponds to the changed circumstances." † This allows the communists to adapt their short-term tactics to the circumstances of the current situation. But it never will permit them to change the basic theory on which the revolution must take place, in accordance with dialectics. And dialectics is simply another word for struggle —for class warfare and violent revolution.

This inflexible theory for the creation of a new communist world completely ignores all individual rights. Despite their constant reference to spiritual ideals, the communists regard the individual man as nothing more than a highly developed animal. The individual is not a separate person, with his own feelings of joy and anguish, but a mere fragment in the idealized concept of "The People" or of "society"—the collective man to which communism is dedicated. Indeed, the materialistic theory of life permits no other conclusion, for it would be destroyed by the recognition of one man's sep-

---

* Dutt, *op. cit.,* Introductory Remarks, p. 19.

† *Ibid.*

arate being and his soul. So would the unchallenged authority of the Communist Party.

Consequently, the use of Pavlovism on human beings is the logical result of communist theory, not an abnormal method of control. Individual jailers and interrogators do not have to be sadists or men with twisted abnormalities to break and dehumanize their captives with scientific calculation. They need only be dedicated communists, or men convinced that they have found an efficient way to maintain power. No problems of conscience disturb them. Their sole concern is fear of their own failure and punishment by the Party. This fear only makes them more determined to accomplish their job. Therefore, no prisoner can divert them from this task by appealing to the ordinary human concepts of right and wrong, or by argument or by persuasion. Similarly, the communist official who demonstrates apparent kindness or softness—particularly after his own or a predecessor's brutality—is not changing his beliefs or his dedication to communism. He merely is using another tactic to achieve the inflexible purpose of destroying his captive's resolve.

The use of this tactic, in fact, was immediately effective in the case of the American prisoners in Korea. Knowing that torture and assassination had been practiced on those captured before them, the GIs expected the same treatment when marched off to prison camps. Instead, they were greeted with soft persuasiveness by communist interpreters, speaking polished and colloquial English. They said the Chinese authorities had no intention of mistreating their prisoners, but merely offered a simple "deal": they only wanted the Americans to listen to their side of the story. Relief over this apparent release from brutality immediately created a liaison between the Americans and their captors; just as the same technique did earlier among the Shanghai Chinese. The prisoners soon discovered, as did the Chinese, that soft reasonableness was only a communist weapon, not a sincere attitude.* It was actually the reward element of Pavlovism.

The same use of reward was continual, of course, in the filthy animal cages of the Shanghai jails where I was kept. And I soon discovered, as did American military prisoners, that a dialogue between jailer and captive was not, as sometimes believed, a debate between men holding opposite ideologies. It was a confrontation between a man of authority, with blind, inflexible devotion to his theory, and an animal under his control. My jailers were no more disposed to consider my thoughts, let alone accept them, than if I were mute.

It is from this attitude that the communists use the beguiling double-talk which often has confused and bewildered free men. They speak of "freedom," but this means guided freedom—guided, or rather controlled, by the Party. They talk of "democracy" but this is a democratic centralism, the dictatorship of the proletariat—under the leadership of the Party. They mention "personal rights," but these are arrogated to the ruling elect; for the individual they mean only the right to follow the Party.† "Human nature" refers not to the individual but to collective man.

To the Chinese communists, the fact that a man has been arrested proves automatically that he is guilty of serious crime. In their legal language they simply do not have a term for a mere "prisoner" or a "suspect" or a "defendant." The only word they use is "fan jen," which means criminal. Interrogators cling to this with fanatic persistence, shouting it endlessly at their captives. Similarly, their legal vocabulary makes no distinction between "sin," "crime," and "mistake." These words also will be repeated constantly in an attempt

---

* Cf. Chap. One, p. 22.

† "On the Correct Handling of Contradictions Among the People," speech by Mao Tse-tung, Feb. 27, 1957, published by New China News Agency, June 18, 1957.

to make the prisoner admit that, perhaps, he has "made a mistake" sometime in the past. An admission of even a simple fault provides the entering wedge for further pressure to force the prisoner to confess that he is a spy or an imperialist. Short of this, the constant reiteration of these charges is part of the continual attempt to wear away resolve and to probe for weaknesses in the mind.

Unless the prisoner wishes to confess, he can accomplish no purpose by discussing his case with the interrogators or, actually, by even talking to them. They cannot be diverted from either their communist philosophy or their effort to break down the prisoner's determination. In this sense, the contest is not one of wits, with persuasion the goal, but of wills, in the starkest sense. Mental well-being often is the stake. The captive who intends to resist must steel himself to fight every minute, against superior odds.

In this guerrilla war of the mind the well-armed man can be confident of ultimate success. But confidence alone cannot replace courage. He must be ready to face isolation and petty indignities which are designed to destroy his self-respect. Physical hardships will be continual. He will be overwhelmed with minute rules and regulations, to befog him and to obscure the reason for his imprisonment. By every means, including the alternation of force and softness, his captors will be raking his soul tirelessly for any sign of weakness, any exploitable doubt. Their endless patience and tireless persistence will tempt him to despair, and the very uncertainty of his fate will fill him with frustration. The Chinese communists are masters at interweaving all these elements into a web to ensnare the unwary. To survive this net of deceit and cruelty unscathed is difficult, but not impossible.

And survival with honor is more than a requirement for everyone involved in the war with the communists, a war that in many ways is more diabolical in prison than in a battle area. It is necessary for the continued self-respect of the survivor himself, for the most abject men I have seen are those who aided the communists, then turned to bitter self-hatred. Brainwashing does not often change a man's thinking, but the acts he commits, while too weak to resist, often alter his thinking about himself. Moreover, my experience shows that cooperation does not necessarily prevent stronger mistreatment, nor does defiance precipitate it. For pragmatic reasons, if no more, resistance is essential.

The man who holds out will survive his experience in better mental and physical condition than if he capitulates.

Inevitably the question is raised: "What is the role of direct physical torture (beatings, the water treatment, electrodes applied to sensitive organs, etc.) in brainwashing?" Here we have a divergence of opinion. For example, Lieutenant Colonel Mayer definitely holds that torture is not an essential part of the process. On the other hand, according to Kinkead, the author of *In Every War But One,** the U.S. army denies that the Korean prisoners underwent brainwashing because no torture was used. Personally I agree with Lieutenant Colonel Mayer, for reasons which I will explain in detail in later chapters.

In actual fact, the Chinese communists used a great deal of physical abuse in the earlier years and seemed to have changed their policy in 1952 or 1953. I believe they modified their system for practical reasons which were by no means humanitarian. They found that subtle psychological pressure combined with continual physical discomfort, oftentimes quite severe, produced better results. At the same time they could shove the foreign prisoners over the border into Hong Kong or Macao without a mark on their bodies. This forestalled much bad publicity abroad, which inevitably cost face for the Chinese. Many people are shocked by scars on a man's

---

* Pp. 17, 31, 32 (W. W. Norton & Co., New York, 1959).

body but pay little heed to the scars on his soul.

Moreover, a man of spirit will be aroused to anger and hostility by a physical beating and show greater resistance. No one could possibly suspect that torturers can become friends, interested in helping the prisoner "solve his case" fairly. Yet not a few succumbed to this illusion under the crafty manipulation of skilled interrogators who did not physically abuse them.

Another puzzling problem is: "Why do the communists go to so much trouble to extort 'genuine confessions' instead of fabricating such documents?" The simple reason is that such confessions have much greater propaganda value. One should not forget that the communists are not chiefly concerned with the prisoner as an individual. They are more interested in using him to confuse and destroy the group which he represents: his family, school, church, military unit, or country. When they succeed in forcing a man to betray himself, they have a powerful propaganda instrument to use against those who are bound to him socially or those among their own people who respect his country or group. In hypocritical self-righteousness, they can say: "This man himself says that he is a criminal. We have only helped him to recognize the evil of his crime. As guardians of public order we would be derelict in our duty if we failed to punish him."

Even if they do not put the "criminal" on public display to recount his crimes, confessions written in the man's own handwriting and style or broadcast by his taped voice create convincing genuineness. And, finally, the query: "Do they use drugs?" In research on this subject, I have never found any clearly credible evidence that the Chinese communists have used drugs. Why should they? They have been successful in achieving their purpose without drugs. If they have drugs that can produce the desired effect, why have they wasted so many years interrogating and indoctrinating their pris-

66

oners? Theoretically at least, they are extremely careful about wasting the workingman's time. And good communist officials pride themselves on belonging to the working class. Surely, if an injection or two could make a man "sing," they would use that timesaving device so that more effort could be spent in reconstructing the New China.

Communist brainwashers use a number of basic techniques against individual prisoners and these are fundamental in all cases. Their methods vary only in detail to meet the diverse attitudes of their captives. Sometimes, in fact, communist authorities appear to "follow the book" even when it proves unproductive. For the purposes of this study, the most important fundamental techniques will be analyzed separately, against my own experience, although the communists seldom rely upon only one weapon at a time.

The indispensable starting point for brainwashing is the immediate attempt to dehumanize the captive. This process began for me on the night of June 15, 1953, when I was swept into jail and lost my membership in the human race.

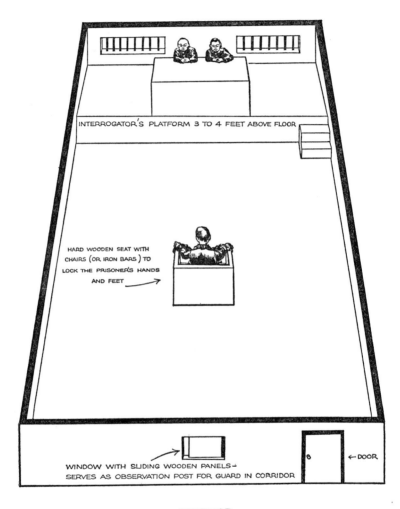

INTERROGATOR'S PLATFORM 3 TO 4 FEET ABOVE FLOOR

HARD WOODEN SEAT WITH CHAIRS (OR IRON BARS) TO LOCK THE PRISONER'S HANDS AND FEET →

WINDOW WITH SLIDING WOODEN PANELS →
SERVES AS OBSERVATION POST FOR GUARD IN CORRIDOR

← DOOR

CORRIDOR

(SIMILAR ROOMS ALONG THE CORRIDOR ON BOTH SIDES)

SKETCH OF ONE OF THE INTERROGATION ROOMS AT SOUTH CITY JAIL

PART TWO

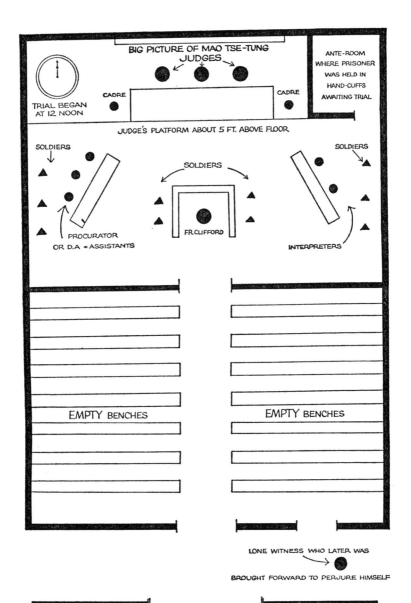

TRIAL BEGAN AT 12 NOON

BIG PICTURE OF MAO TSE-TUNG

JUDGES

CADRE

CADRE

ANTE-ROOM WHERE PRISONER WAS HELD IN HAND-CUFFS AWAITING TRIAL

JUDGE'S PLATFORM ABOUT 5 FT. ABOVE FLOOR.

SOLDIERS

SOLDIERS

SOLDIERS

PROCURATOR OR D.A + ASSISTANTS

FR. CLIFFORD

INTERPRETERS

EMPTY BENCHES

EMPTY BENCHES

LONE WITNESS WHO LATER WAS BROUGHT FORWARD TO PERJURE HIMSELF

TRIAL SCENE AT SHANGHAI DISTRICT COURT DURING FR. CLIFFORD'S "TRIAL"

Chapter four

DELIBERATE
DE-HUMANIZING

IN THE DANK SILENCE MY LACELESS SHOES
noisily slapped the hard pavement. Shoelaces and my belt
had been taken from me, along with other possessions, when
I entered the prison office a few minutes earlier. Now, walking down the narrow corridor between cells, the sound of
those loose shoes seemed to epitomize my helplessness. With
one hand I clutched my slipping pants and with the other
I clung to a thin bundle of clothing. The dignity with which
I had promised myself to accept imprisonment seemed to be
a delusion.

Following the guard, I could sense the disdain in his square,
thick shoulders, as he padded almost noiselessly in his cloth
shoes. A feeble electric bulb, high in the ceiling, scattered
tired beams of light on iron-barred doors, each completely

covered with wooden planks. I could not see into the cells. The guard hurried ahead as if anxious to be finished with the trip. I stumbled after him as best I could.

My arrest, at 11:30 P.M. on June 15, 1953, had been a perfunctory climax to four years of waiting. Almost daily, since the communists occupied Shanghai, I had expected the police to take me. They performed this task as gruffly and as unimaginatively as I had anticipated, yet when it was accomplished I felt a gray fog of uncertainty for which I had been unable to prepare myself. As I was driven to Loukawei prison —barely ten minutes from my church—I realized that I had to fight constantly against any thoughts of gloom for myself or others, or be lost. The best defense, I thought, was to maintain human dignity.

But the prison authorities had anticipated that. From the beginning they treated me like the lowest, most common criminal. I was stripped, and my body and clothing thoroughly searched. The priceless trifles I had brought—my rosary and prayer book—were confiscated, along with eyeglasses, watch, and $7,000 in Chinese currency (worth at that time about 35 cents U.S.), to be held for my release. My name was taken also, and I was handed a small piece of cloth with my new identity—No. 774. When ordered to re-dress, I was deprived of all articles that might be used for suicide; as if I had ever faintly believed that arrest was not inevitable.

These routine criminal practices normally are carried out in a Chinese prison with contempt for the individual which would be depressing to any Westerner; particularly the innocent. But the communists have given them new indignity. To this is added the realization that the communists have absolute control over the prisoner, with no legal or moral restraints. Moreover, the authorities made it clear that my "crimes" were heinous when they spat the charges out to me. I was a "saboteur" and an "imperialist."

The guard stopped midway down the corridor and looked back at me impatiently. Somewhere behind the wooden walls a low moan started, then was smothered quickly. The thick, breathless silence returned. I shuffled ahead.

Finally, we stopped at the end of the corridor before Cell No. 1. The door creaked open, and I was shoved inside. Instantly, the door clanged behind me. Then—silence.

A tiny, dirty bulb covered the cell with dusty light. Five Chinese, lumped beneath blankets on the floor, turned lifeless eyes toward me. If the sight of a foreign priest made any difference to them, none showed it. One by one the eyes closed and, without moving, my cellmates pretended sleep. There was not a sound. But, in the boarded stagnation of the cell, the smells were alive—unwashed clothing, the heavy breath of half-sleep, the lavatory, a wooden bucket at my feet. Where was my dignity now?

A narrow slit, face-high in the door, clicked open. Turning, I could see a slice of the guard's face, and his crooked, stained teeth. "Hey, you criminals," he shouted, "move over and give him room!"

The human lumps stirred reluctantly. The farthest man rolled over a few inches and pulled his thin mat with him. Each of the others did the same. They left me a space of about eight inches at the end, next to the bucket, so I spread the thin mat and the blanket I had snatched off my bed when arrested and lay down on the wooden floor. The light bulb glared at me, and for many hours I stared back . . .

It seemed as if a sudden explosion awakened me, but it was only the guard banging reveille on the wooden door with his club. It was about 5 A.M. The cell looked the same as the night before, for the barred window also had been covered with wood and the morning light was too feeble to push through the cracks. The electric bulb still glared, as I glanced swiftly around. The cell was about 12 feet long and 6 feet wide, a plain box with a door at one end.

My cellmates rose listlessly and silently. Carefully they arranged their blankets, adjusted their straw mats on the floor; then, still silently, sat on the floor, with their backs against the wall. I followed their example. For half an hour we leaned against the clammy wall, preoccupied with our nothingness. None of the others showed any interest in me or in each other. They merely sat staring at the filthy floor. My mind was busy wondering what the authorities were going to do with me.

Then the peephole clicked and two of the prisoners rose quickly and left the cell. They returned with two basins of water, and we took turns washing in it; with what, I thought at the time, was a marvelous display of prison hygiene. I was last, of course, and the water was grimy when it reached me. There was time to notice that these strange men took extra care to avoid spillage on the dirty floor; well-advised caution, I was to learn later.

For another two and one-half hours, we became human islands again, propped against the wall. The silence was startling. These were average Chinese, who looked as if they shared the national love for conversation. Yet at that point they observed with fidelity the cardinal prison prohibition against talking. Moreover, they appeared to be so used to the injunction that they no longer resented or resisted it. So they sat, staring ahead; sallow men, with ragged clothes and ragged souls.

At another signal, a third prisoner disappeared through the creaking door, returning with a pan of rice and a pan of vegetables. We were given tin rice bowls and chopsticks, and the food was divided among us. A guard, barking through the peephole, ordered us to eat as quickly as possible. When we had gulped the dry rice and a sliver of cabbage, the guard opened the door again. Jumping quickly, the prisoner on

KP duty—a "privileged by merit" trusty—stacked the bowls in one of the basins. Then, with nervous obsequiousness, he showed the whole array to the guard, standing menacingly in front of him.

"See," the prisoner said, "not one grain of the people's rice has been wasted."

The prisoners immediately folded themselves back into position to hold up the wall. Then I discovered the reason for this unnatural, unhuman behavior. A long printed list of "Rules for Criminals" was posted on one wall. All of the waking hours, it said, were to be spent by the "criminal" in meditating on his "crimes"—from 5:00 A.M. to 9:00 P.M. In addition to strictly forbidding any conversation, the rules specified that the prisoner must sit on the floor with his back to the wall in a place designated by the guard. He must not move from this spot, except occasionally to shift arms and legs. No reading material was available. No smoking.

There were more rules. When speaking to a guard, or any other official, they said, the criminal should come to attention. He should then listen respectfully and answer in a low tone. No criminal should accept any material object, such as soap, towel, clothing or food, from another prisoner. Everyone should remain silent about his name and former life. It was strictly forbidden to discuss the "reason" for imprisonment, and a prisoner revealing this would be harshly punished.

The instructions also specified that "confession" should be complete. The sooner this was done, and the more thorough the confession, the shorter and easier would be the sentence. After oral confession, the prisoner was to write his admission under the direction of the judges. When he had satisfied the judges that all past wrongdoing had been acknowledged he could gain "merit" by informing them of the "errors" of his relatives, friends or acquaintances outside of prison. He could also gain merit by informing on fellow prisoners.

All criminals, the rules added, must make an extreme effort to advance in their political and social reeducation. When discussions were allowed in the cells, the prisoner should do all he possibly could to help a cellmate "reform" his thinking and adopt a "positive attitude" toward the people's government.

Any infraction of these rules, it was emphasized, would be considered counterrevolutionary and would result in "severe punishment." The death penalty was added, in 1955, a year before my release, for prisoners refusing to confess or to cooperate.

The officials had informed me that the rules were designed for the "good of the criminal," for they were a guiding path toward a "new life." Those who abided faithfully by these regulations would be handled leniently.

It was evident from my first glimpse of these harsh orders, in the apathetic silence that morning, that they were intended with clever thoroughness to make each prisoner completely dependent upon the state, and as quickly as possible. Absolute obedience was expected and, in Mao's mythology, this was the only way for a criminal to obtain sufficient merit to be classified once more as a "person." Guards, interrogators and judges all were representatives of the people's government. Prisoners immediately became dependent upon them to move a muscle, even to go to the bathroom. Group solidarity among the captives was broken before it could form, for it was specified that any attempt to curry favor with another prisoner would be considered as an affront to the "providence" of the government; a serious crime.

Everything fitted the grand design—the indignities, the boarded cells, the glaring light, and the long list of childish rules. It was clear that the rules would be rigidly enforced, for they were fundamental to this dehumanization. The regulations were so primitive that they immediately made every-

76

thing dependent on trivia; reducing men to an existence that, by edict, approached the animal. The communist authorities —from guards to judges—were ingenious in enforcing the spirit as well as the letter of these rules.

As I absorbed the meaning of this calculated pettiness, the guard banged his club on the door. My cellmates jumped quickly upright, and I followed. Then, in a ragged line, we were marched down the empty hall to a filthy bathroom at the end. Care was taken that no one else could see us, and the trip was made at what might be called top speed. Back in the cell, we sat once more.

That was the routine within our cage. Twice a day we marched down the hall and back again. Occasionally we were permitted to walk around in the cell, to ease aching muscles. We were fed in the morning and again in late afternoon, and after each so-called meal were given a cup of hot water. All else was silent vegetation.

It was easy to see that erosion already had begun among my cellmates. Their faces had become waxen and purposefully expressionless. I was unable to catch any of them smiling at his thoughts or frowning or displaying even a shadow of anger. For several days they regarded me with a common mask of suspicion, for I had become the odd man who might also be the cell informer. They had only two other masks—fright and servility.

Suddenly I realized how important it was to fight debilitation every moment. The acceptance of any part of this treatment without mental revolt would mean weakening all resistance to the rest of it. Once a man conceded that, in fact, he had become animalistic, each step toward total capitulation would become easier; and, conversely, resisting it would be progressively more difficult. The loss of human dignity was designed to be so thorough and so shocking by itself, I decided, that it would overshadow all else. If a prisoner could be made to lose confidence in himself as a human being, if he came to regard filth and coarse discipline as normal or even acceptable, how significant to him would be the confession of an imaginary crime? But his confession would be forever the brand of the greatest crime, the renunciation of his dignity as a human being. A man's soul had been given him to defend him from its enemies.

So I resolved to fight back with the only weapon the state could not take away—myself. I could be made to live like an animal, but I could not be reduced to the same mental level —provided that I held under tight control my mind, my will, my emotions. I prayed that morning, silently, for the strength to fight for my soul, no matter what the ordeal.

It was in this mood that I began my vigil of the wooden floor. Up to then my life in Shanghai had been enjoyable, active, interesting and stimulating. Despite the communist regime and the sorrows it inflicted on those around me, I had felt a sense of purpose and accomplishment. My work had become a cherished obligation and I was never really alone. Now, friends and colleagues had been torn away and I was thrust into isolation—for how long? The realization gave me a moment of panic, I confess, and I know how quickly despair can come.

Then, in my first victory, I decided to devote these hours to so many thoughts that time again would be too short for all I wanted to do. First, I had to plan my counterattack with care and thoroughness, going over it repeatedly, so there would be no mistake. This eventually became a game, to see how I could outwit my captors in my mind, and later in person. Second, I made a ritual of recalling all the pleasant events of my life, all the joys and laughter and, most of all, the moments when my will had triumphed over weakness. In time I could sense the dawn and smell a rose and hear the laughter of my mother, while the cell grew more fetid and the electric bulb more garish. Finally, I stretched out my prayers and my meditation so that they became a dominant part of each morning; a measure of faith peculiar to a priest but denied to no one.

In this mood I began to welcome the mental leisure, free from the normal pressures of life and the requirements of more than sixteen years of scheduled demands. There was no bustle to prepare for classes or to write sermons or to hurry through the list of books demanding to be read in numbers too great for one man's capacity. I did not have to plunge into the scrambled traffic of the city, at risk of limb and nervous system, or survive the endless pyramid of petty annoyances that formed a day of achievement. It no longer was necessary to endure what, for me, was the daily ordeal of shaving or wearing hot, tight clothes in broiling weather.

If all this was delusion, it was lifesaving delusion, formed piece by piece in my mind. The physical task of sitting almost immobile on the hard floor competed for my attention. Until I developed calluses in the correct places, my stern section seemed to be boring through the floor with white heat. The pain was excruciating. As my bones jellified under the pressure, the pain shot up my back, into my shoulders and into a mind ever eager for distraction from the task of thinking. Leg muscles began to atrophy, or so it seemed, and they protested when I moved them cautiously, to avoid the guard's attention, or when I hugged my knees to straighten out the kinks. The impulse to jump up and run or try breaking through the door became almost irresistible; a constantly nagging pressure which grew stronger each day and became another dragon to slay.

The communists knew these feelings, so they enforced immobility with thoroughness. They knew, too, the capacity of the mind, and since the mind was their enemy they attacked it directly, without relying upon the slower corrosion of vegetation. All day, and most of the night, the guards in our block of twelve cells were busy tending their cages.

One pair was particularly efficient or, perhaps, more frightened than the others over censure from the Party. The dominant member of this unwholesome team was a thin, wiry country boy from Shantung province; no more than five feet four inches tall, and a bare 130 pounds. He was sharp-featured, with high cheekbones and a prominent nose, so mentally I nicknamed him the Mole. Hate and suspicion smoldered in his slitted eyes, and he had the most stentorian voice I ever heard. His frequent partner, another Shantung peasant, became the Horse in my mind; a rugged, well-proportioned man of about 170 pounds, standing perhaps five feet eight inches. His strong, square face and jutting chin reflected devotion rather than intellect, and if there was no hatred in his eyes, neither was there mercy. His voice was a window-shaking bray.

The Mole intruded into my careful mental isolation as I was taking a swim at a California beach on one particularly stifling afternoon. The cell had rippled momentarily when one of the Chinese prisoners returned from interrogation at the headquarters office elsewhere in the prison. Eyes downcast and face hammered into an expressionless mask, the prisoner dropped into his groove on the floor and allowed his chin to slump forward. The rest of us returned to mental droning.

Suddenly the door slit shot open and the Mole, who was scarcely tall enough to see through it, bellowed, "Hey, you!"

The returned prisoner shot back his head, and his eyes widened in fright.

"Yes, I mean you—fan jen—criminal," the Mole roared, in the whipsawing tones of the Mandarin dialect. "Caught you sleeping in the daytime. Don't you know that is a crime against the people?"

80

The prisoner, a haggard old man with ribs for cheekbones, started to shake his head, then caught himself and remained still, mouth half-open.

"Don't deny it!" the Mole shouted. "You are guilty. Admit it, ungrateful pig!"

"But, sir . . ."

"Shut up. Come here!"

The prisoner stumbled upright and shuffled toward the door, stopping with his face pressed tightly to the peephole. This was the approved position, after a summons from the guard, so that the prisoner could talk without being heard; therefore enforcing his isolation from the group and his dependence upon the people's representative. The old man knew it well, for he had been imprisoned for more than a year. At the peephole he made a pathetic attempt to straighten his thin shoulders into attention, but the gesture looked more like a helpless shrug.

All the while he stood there a frightened nerve in his scrawny neck twitched and hammered against leathery skin. Yet somewhere inside him the man retained a flicker of defiance. It was evident he had not satisfied his inquisitors during the earlier interrogation, and the Mole had been ordered to continue the treatment.

"You running dog of the imperialists," the guard began, his face sneering through the peephole, a few inches from his victim, "you decadent capitalist. Admit your crime. You were asleep."

The prisoner murmured something, unintelligible to us but obviously unacceptable to the Mole.

"Counterrevolutionary!" the midget dictator screamed. "Oppressor of the people! Admit you were asleep!"

Again a murmur. Again the epithets. The shopworn communist phrases became curses, more stinging than any filthy word. With the hypocritical puritanism affected by the communists the Mole avoided normal Chinese profanity.

For at least fifteen minutes the Mole screamed with increasing frenzy and uninterrupted venom. Noisy belittlement represents power in Asia, and power is measured by the viciousness of tone and the inability of the victim to respond in kind. This twisted, frustrated little guard was driven by something inside him, perhaps, to demonstrate his power.

"Bloodsucking capitalist"! he finally snapped, and left. The prisoner remained standing, glued to the peephole. The sudden silence was itself another curse. Tightened nerves barely had time to unravel, however, before the Mole was back, refreshed and recharged. He continued his tirade, with infrequent pauses, for another three hours, until the end of his four-hour shift. When the prisoner finally stumbled back to sanctuary on the floor, his eyes were glazed and, I could see, another layer of resolve had been peeled away.

When the Mole and the Horse had overlapping shifts, this treatment sometimes continued without interruption for the solid eight hours. The victim would be drawn indiscriminately from one of the twelve cells, and no matter who he was, the crashing epithets of the guards could be heard throughout the cellblock, as planned. Between formal tirades the browbeating continued, if on a lesser plane. Our peephole played a constant tune, as the people's representatives took turns to see whether the rules of the state were being observed to the letter. Permission had to be obtained even to use the bucket, and the state condescended to grant this privilege only after a rasping repetition of cursing dogma. The long parade of guards, who carried out these nation-building duties at Loukawei and the three other prisons I graced, never faltered in their combined devotion to detail; although a few of them appeared to be unimpressed by the whole performance.

At night we lined up for formal permission to lie on the

hard floor and the attempt to ease the tensions that had been built during the ordeal of living through the sixteen-hour day shift. It usually took me more than an hour to relax enough to attempt sleep. All the while the light glared into my face, and frequently, unfriendly eyes would be watching through the peephole. Finally the herd would settle down in the cell, and exhaustion would take over.

When that had been achieved, almost every night, oblivion would be broken by a heavy cannon shot, reverberating through the confined cell and tangling nerves again. The sudden shock was almost enough to lift me off the floor each time.

The fusillade was only the guard banging his club on the gonglike door. He would do this to tell a prisoner to move over and give more room to a neighbor. He would bang to inform a man that he was snoring. Often he shot us awake for no announced reason. But the purpose was clear, for fatigue is a calculated element of Pavlovism, and idle men must be forced into physical, as well as mental, exhaustion. This treatment was so thorough that, in three years' imprisonment, I had only one night of complete rest.

One night sleep was particularly elusive and when I dozed off it was after midnight. Suddenly a new sound jerked me into a sitting crouch. Somewhere in the cellblock a prisoner was screaming in terror. Over and over he shouted in French, "I refuse. I refuse! I protest in the name of the Catholics of the whole world."

Several guards must have been with him, for the noise of shuffling feet was loud. Then I heard the Mole shout, "Use your gun! Use your gun!"—apparently as a club. There was a scuffle, the crack of blows, a heavy thud. The scrape of chains echoed along the passageway, followed by the heavier sounds of an object being dragged across the rough floor; perhaps a body. The poor man evidently was a French priest who had been questioned and did not give the proper answers.

At first the episode seemed like a nightmare. But I was awake, for I could see the glaring light and I could smell the bucket. My cellmates were awake, too, and their drawn faces showed that they also were terrified.

Yet, as the days wore on, we dreaded to be ignored almost as much as we dreaded the sounds of abuse that came regularly to our sharpened ears. Whenever the outside door to our cellblock would open, I could sense the tenseness among my cellmates, a tenseness that I experienced as well. The thought in each mind was: Are they coming for *me*, now? To some, this anticipation no doubt was unpleasant, for they pictured further harsh scenes with the interrogators. It was apparent, however, that two of my companions—the "trusties" who brought food and water—had begun to accept the false belief that, with further confession, they might solve their cases and win enough merit for release.

Whenever the outer door opened, these two became particularly alert. When the guard's footsteps passed our cell, they whispered their disappointment to each other. Mumbled conversations became possible on occasions when one of the guards was absent from the cellblock, and the prisoners frequently took advantage of the situation. Moreover, the guards seemed more willing to overlook the transgressions of these two men; a sign that they were becoming "progressive"—the euphemism for cooperation with the authorities, or capitulation. These two were indistinguishable outwardly from the other Chinese, but inside they were made of different stuff.

On another stifling morning they responded typically, when the outer door clanged open and footsteps pounded toward us. The door of our cell creaked. The sergeant of the guard, a thin young man in a civilian suit, came in, insolently smoking a cigarette. As we jumped to attention, the progressives

84

looked almost eager, while the rest of us adjusted the mask of impassiveness. The sergeant haughtily surveyed his ragged command, blew a puff of tantalizing smoke into the cell and barked an order.

A couple of soldiers immediately entered and began pawing through the small bundles of clothing and personal possessions at each man's place. They untied the piece of cloth in which these items were packed and methodically pulled out every T shirt, every ragged sock, and every shirt. This was supposed to be an inspection for hidden weapons or counterrevolutionary material; as if we could miraculously obtain these things within our tightly enclosed packing box. When each article had been patted and shaken, it was tossed indiscriminately onto a heap on the floor. Soon everyone's possessions were heaped together in the center of the cell, and separation would be another tedious process. The progressives could not hide disappointment when their own clothes went into the same pile. A single command had put them back, at least momentarily, to our level. The sergeant, meanwhile, calmly finished his cigarette, flipped it aimlessly toward a makeshift cuspidor on the floor, then glared contemptuously at each man in turn. Without a word, he turned and left, with the soldiers after him, abandoning the mess.

After each of these trifling incidents, as well as more chilling events, you could feel the letdown in the cell. Even in silence, the erosion of hope and the weakening of determination became tangible and detectable. Soon I was convinced that little in this prison happened by chance, but that nearly everything was part of a plan, carefully devised and scrupulously executed. This filthy, smelly, stuffy hole was intended to be a pigsty, and we were animals penned up for experimentation. The minor irritations were deliberate. So was the fact that the rice fed to us frequently contained small, white rocks. When ordered to eat as fast as possible, we gulped the rocks as well as the rice. As a result, I broke three teeth during my confinement. Fortunately, the teeth did not bother me until after I had left prison.

Life was distilled almost overnight to minutiae, all of which were manipulated to increase our isolation from normality and to reduce us to automatic response. When the communists pressed the button, we all were supposed to jump. This kind of existence is what the psychologists call a controlled environment, designed to produce autoreaction. In other words, this was intended as the first step toward the conditioned reflexes of Pavlovism.

Systematic manipulation of these trivia was calculated to lead us to discouragement, frustration, helpless dependence upon our captors, confusion of mind and debilitation of spirit. The combination of minor vexations can reach the point where the prisoner is likely to forget the main reason for his imprisonment. Out of befuddlement and sheer frustration, he may react so automatically to command or pressure that he might confess almost anything—even uncommitted crimes—to escape further accusation or torment.

The dictionary may not list such trifling events as I have described as torture, but as the weeks, months and years roll by they can undermine a man's spirit and turn him virtually into a creature of instinct. Moreover, the screams in the night, the constant threats of interrogators, and known history convince him that direct brutality and torture are always possible for every prisoner. As he is conditioned to minutiae, he is conditioned also to the reality that communists, driven by inflexible purpose, have absolute control over his treatment and his fate.

Watching lifelessness and helplessness creep across the faces of my cellmates, I intensified my efforts to break from the environment through mental flight. Where there was no sunlight, I could bring back at will the golden sparkle of the sea near San Francisco. Where there was no darkness, I could feel the soft blackness of a night in the woods. Where there was only bestiality and meanness, I could revive the intellectual challenge of the campus at the University of Santa Clara, where I had taught philosophy before coming to China.

I reread all my favorite books in my mind and struggled again with canon law. Through long afternoons I went back through the principles of dialectical materialism, which I had studied years before in college, and found them no more valid or correct when turned against me than when analyzed logically. Quarter by quarter I replayed the twenty-game schedule of our star high school football team when, for two years, no opponent scored on us. It was a great team, and I was a proud little character on the bench. Weighing about 150 pounds, I had fought hard for a regular berth at guard in a line of comparative giants. Curiously, I could still feel the disappointment over my failures to make the first team. I remembered, too, the years of high school and college debating, when we tackled the world's great problems with youthful enthusiasm and misinformation. As a rebuttal specialist, I had acquired a reputation for backing any opponent into a corner; perhaps through sheer stubbornness.

The one window in our packing-case cell had been boarded completely, but a careless workman had left a few cracks. On fair days the sun sifted through them and slanted across the far wall. As it marched upward toward the ceiling and extinction, I learned to tell the hours. The days were measured by prison routine.

On Sundays there seldom were any interrogations, and the time was spent in makeshift efforts by the trusties to clean the prison. The seasons blew in on us.

My sense of isolation was intensified by the fact that the prison was only a short distance from my own church (Christ the King), while St. Peter's Church was only five minutes' walk away. I could easily recall the busy streets around these familiar landmarks, but their clamor largely was cut off, even from our prison-sharpened ears. Occasionally we could hear the hum of traffic and, when the wind was right, I caught the early-morning peal of bells at St. Peter's.

Putting these fragments together, I was able eventually to determine the date of Easter each year. The communists obviously gave no sign of recognizing the first Sunday after the first full moon after the 21st of March. But they permitted the Chinese people to celebrate their traditional New Year's holiday, if somewhat desultorily. The noise of the usual firecrackers penetrated the prison, telling me that the date was late January. Fifteen days later the moon would be full. With a little juggling of the lunar and solar calendars and a bit of guesswork I was able to work out the complicated formula. My calculations were a week off the first year but accurate thereafter, as I learned by checking back with the calendar after my release. In all this welcome time-consuming concern with Easter, however, I was unprepared for one of the joking questions asked me after my return to the United States. "Father," said a sweet young thing, "what did you give up for Lent?"

These mental gymnastics were lifesaving. But, as time ground into me, I realized that I was only holding my own and that I had to make a more direct counterattack against my tormentors. Otherwise I would remain stagnant, even though avoiding retrogression. Perhaps the communist authorities realized this, too. They ignored me for weeks after my imprisonment, in what evidently was a deliberate reminder that I could rot in the pigstay.

I had worked out detailed counterstrategy in my mind and had devised elaborate and separate programs for repaying the Mole and the Horse for their varied kindnesses.

By necessity, these tactics were based upon the use of trivia against those who had made them dominant in our lives. I had no other weapons. In fact, knowing communist inflexibility over their own doctrine, I doubted whether they could be affected by any prisoner except on the basis of their own pettiness; a point that was later confirmed fully. But I began to doubt whether I would get the chance to use this strategy, and my restlessness increased. The fight back from vegetation necessarily creates an intense desire to lash out, if only verbally, at captors.

My first chance came the day I dropped a single grain of rice on the floor of the filthy cell. The Mole was watching through the peephole. When the tiny particle slipped off my chopstick, he roared loudly enough to rattle the bars.

"Pick it up," he screamed, "and eat it."

"No!" I shouted.

"Pick it up, capitalist. That is the food of the people's democratic government. It cannot be wasted. Eat it!"

"No," I continued, in Mandarin. "The people's democratic government is taking care of me. It wants me to preserve my health. I would not want to disappoint the people's democratic government by eating rice that is full of germs, and by falling sick."

The guard brayed momentarily with impotent rage. Like many others, he was infected with the superstitious nonsense of germ warfare which Peking was still spreading.

"You American capitalist-imperialist," he finally shouted. "You are wasting the blood and sweat of our poor farmers. Pick it up!"

Deliberately I leaned over, picked up the rice, walked over to the bucket and threw it in.

The Mole roared again. He called me back to the door and cursed me with every slogan he could recall. But he gave up after a few minutes, and I went back happily to reverie.

89

A few days later, on a damp, feverish morning, the peephole suddenly cracked open when I was completing my usual prayers. The Horse called me to the door and asked me why my lips were moving.

"I'm praying," I answered.

The Horse galloped into a shouting rage. With the usual preliminary dialectical insults, he accused me of violating the rule against talking, by moving my lips.

I yelled back at him, with Irish enthusiasm.

"I have my rules as a Catholic priest, and you have yours as a communist. You obey your rules—and I'll obey mine."

The screaming match began then in earnest, and despite the rules, I shouted as loudly as he did. I wanted the entire cellblock to know that I was there and why I was there. Whenever he stopped for breath, I took up the tirade. In detail, I described the persecution of the Church under the communists and told everybody about the slow starvation and murder of many foreign and Chinese priests in Shanghai. In reply, the guard merely increased the venom of his insults.

After nearly an hour of this, the guard told me to stand where I was, and slammed the peephole. The cell was apprehensively silent behind me, and I felt a chill of concern over what might happen next. But I also was exhilarated and confident.

In a few minutes the Horse returned with the sergeant of the guard. With a final, fragrant puff of smoke the sergeant threw away his cigarette at the door and strode into the cell, shouting and waving his arms. He thrust his arrogant face into mine and continued to shout. I looked up at him, for I was a couple of inches shorter, and purposefully kept my eyes steady.

"You pig," the sergeant yelled, "you bloodsucking capitalist. You have broken the rules. Admit it!"

"I have done only what it is my right to do," I retorted.

"Criminal! You have no rights. Only the Party has rights.

You are nothing."

"I have rights as a human being," I shouted.

"Bah! Capitalist nonsense!" Then he spit in my face. With an effort, I held myself still, although I could feel the blood pounding in my head.

The sergeant continued to scream for perhaps another half hour. His lips were drawn into a thin, angry line, and a vein in his forehead pounded with excitement.

"You have broken the rules," he repeated finally. "Admit it! We can make you admit it!"

"I have broken no rules," I shouted. "You had no right to arrest me. You have no rights over me. And I will continue to pray."

"Is that so, criminal? We shall see. Wait there." He swung around and marched out.

In the cell, bottled breath escaped with a soft hiss. But I felt more confident than at any time since my arrest. As I had anticipated during my long mental strategy sessions, the communists had begun to show their inability to handle any prisoner reaction except the one they expected. Defiance and shouting certainly were unexpected. The punishment of standing at attention was actually welcome to me, at the moment, for anything was better than agonizing immobility on the floor.

I stood there for at least an hour. Gradually the situation began to appear increasingly humorous, and I chuckled inwardly. This was, to say the least, hardly a West Point parade. Standing at attention, communist style, meant clutching the pants with one hand to keep them in place. The baggy and odorous trousers permitted me to bend my knees slightly, when convenient and desirable. Laceless shoes were loose, and I could move my toes freely. No sloppier recruit ever tried coming to attention.

Finally, the peephole opened again, and I could see the

lined, worried face of the warden, a man of great power in this human laboratory.

"What is the trouble?" he asked, in rather moderate tones.

"I am being persecuted because of my religion," I replied, loudly and clearly.

Bang went the peephole.

Half an hour later it opened again. "You are a criminal," the warden began, more harshly, "an imperialist. You will be severely punished unless you admit your faults."

"What faults? Being a priest?"

The peephole closed immediately.

The authorities let me stand there for several more hours. Then a guard—a new guard—told me to sit down. I was not bothered again, on this issue or at this time. The Horse, who had started it all, disappeared and was never seen again in our cellblock.

Childish? Perhaps, but also momentous. The communists had imprisoned me on the political charges of being an imperialist and a saboteur and they wanted those charges to stick and to assume general validity. In their method of doing things, this was a matter of considerable significance, but they could not permit any inference that I had been arrested as a priest or was being held for religious reasons. This also was a matter of importance to them.

I had exposed the first weakness, and the incident convinced me that I could use the religious argument whenever tension reached a point where I had to blow off steam. But the fight was just beginning.

Chapter five

INTIMIDATION
AND FORCE

THE DAY FOLLOWING THE DEBATE ON RE-
ligion I was ordered from the cell for my first formal
interrogation. The guard yelled for me with unusual brusqueness and kept his Luger pistol trained on me as I stumbled
from the cellblock and into an open courtyard. There I reveled
in the golden splash of sunlight and the fresh air, which
carried the comforting murmur of street noises. This contact
with the outside world lasted only a few seconds, but it had
a bracing effect.

Like all the other thousands of communist prisoners, I
faced this moment with greatly varied emotions. There was
apprehension, of course, for I did not know what to expect,
and my capacity for enduring pain was no greater than average. Yet I knew I had to avoid making any confession or

93

admission, at all costs. Before arrest, I had promised my students I would not write a statement of any sort and never would sign my name to a confession. I had taught them to resist the communist violation of man, but how could I expect them to remain steadfast if I capitulated? Moreover, any discussion of my relations with my Chinese friends and students, or any unguarded admission, might give the authorities the clues they needed to arrest and persecute them. Equally important was my sense of deep obligation to my country, for I had seen at first hand the impact of American confessions.

The guard barked and his pistol pointed the way into an adjoining building and up the stairs. We entered a large, plain room which had a high ceiling and a general air of neglect. The bare whitewashed walls were stained and weather-beaten. At one end two curtainless unwashed French doors served as windows. Now wide open, they admitted the clamor and the odors of the streets below. The interrogator, a young, rather pleasant-faced man, sat behind a wooden table, which held only an ashtray, some teacups, and the unmistakable cardboard folder of a dossier. A plain chair in front of him and another chair for the uniformed guard— whose Luger seemed to be a foot long—completed the furniture.

The whole effect was drab impermanence, as if interrogation had been only a temporary phase of a military emergency. The drabness showed that. While engaged in this activity, the communist officials accepted the Spartan discomforts they were encouraging their people to adopt. It was an effective stage set.

The interrogator waved an invitation for me to sit down. Then he stared at me momentarily with sharp, quizzical eyes. Tapping the folder with a thin, soft finger, he explained that it contained a complete record of my seven years in China.

"It seems," he began politely, "that you have misunderstood the reasons for your imprisonment. You are here because of crimes you have committed against the people, and not because of your religion."

"I . . ."

"Never mind. We have all the facts we need to prove your guilt. All we want is verification of a few minor points. So I would like a complete résumé of your life, particularly the period in China. Take your time."

The interrogator—or judge, as these officials often are called —settled back for a long siege. Politely, I began recounting all the the antiseptic details I could recall. It was evident from the interrogator's manner and his incisive questions that the authorities expected me to follow the usual pattern. They counted upon dehumanization and vegetation to create such frustrations that the prisoner would be eager to talk and to reveal slight but incriminating facts about himself; if for no other reason than to reestablish his identity as a human being. But my self-censored biography required only the comparatively short period of a couple of hours.

When I had finished, the interrogator looked at me as if expecting more. I made it clear that the story was complete, and the judge instantly dropped his mask of politeness. Slamming his hands on the desk, he shouted angrily, "You are lying. You have not told the whole story. You have not revealed the crimes you have committed."

I calmly replied, "I have no crimes. You are the criminal. You arrested me. I did not arrest you."

"You are in jail because you are a criminal," the interrogator yelled.

"You are the criminal!" I retorted sharply. "You are persecuting me because of my religion, and that is a crime."

Instantly the guard rushed at me with drawn pistol. The judged jumped to his feet, pushing back his chair, then motioned the guard away. "Stand up!" he screamed at me. "You are in the People's Court, and you must show respect for it."

"I have committed no crimes," I insisted, "and I refuse to discuss my past life with you any longer—or any other subjects." From then on I remained silent.

The interrogator lectured me angrily for another half hour, standing at his desk, pacing the room, thrusting a finger into my face. He repeated all the familiar slogan-epithets and all the threadbare charges.

"We have ways to make you talk," he said at last, "and we do not hesitate to use them."

I was thankful that the baggy pants hid my trembling knees, for the threats were real enough. The cellblock guards frequently had showed me the rusty handcuffs they used on other prisoners, and the clank of the leg chains had become a familiar sound. I had heard the beating of the terrified French priest in an adjacent cell. In the outside world we had received confirmed details of the torture and death of Father Bede Chang, a gentle, wise Chinese priest. We knew the story of a 75-year-old French Jesuit, whose unmarked body was delivered to his Superior after three weeks' imprisonment. An American friend of mine, another priest, had been kept for months in a wooden box too small to permit him to stand erect, to sit or to lie down.

If there is a decisive first moment of truth in such a situation, it must be when the vision of all the communist horror is evoked by the threat to use it against the individual who must make his own decision. I was frightened and apprehensive, while the judge snapped at my nerves, but at that second I also turned more stubborn and more determined.

Along with faith, I was sustained by the proof that my countertactics were working. Events were confirming my belief that extreme punishment was not necessarily spontaneous and depended less on the interplay of cooperation and opposition than on other factors. I had defied the authorities twice, directly and rather crudely, without being beaten.

The judge abruptly dismissed me after a final outburst of threats, and I was returned to the cell. During the next eighteen days the pressure was intensified against me and those around me. I was summoned half a dozen times to the same interrogation room, and on each occasion the guard seemed particularly gruff and hostile, so that I could only expect the worst. At the start of each interrogation, I repeated my standard phrase, "Not guilty," then remained absolutely quiet. Forced to stand at attention, I endured hours of epithets and slogans and boring dogma. New interrogators took over the task, and the first judge disappeared; a sign that he had temporarily lost face. Each new judge took pains to repeat the same vague threats of torture, in the general but ominous phrases preferred by communists.

During these long, tedious and often frightening sessions, I conditioned myself to summon mental escape. By adamantly refusing to talk at all I saved my strength and avoided the wearing necessity of guarding my statements to prevent a slip that might prove valuable to my tormentors. When the invective became almost unbearable, I reached for more courage by recalling the comforting quotation: "Do not be afraid when you are called upon by magistrates and judges." Or, perhaps: "I will be with you all days, even till the end of time." Once, my arms were handcuffed tightly behind me for six hours, while the interrogator repeated over and over, "Your case will never be solved unless you confess." And my mind responded stanchly: "I can do all things in Him who strengthens me." At last I wore out the judge, and impatiently he sent me away.

In the cellblock the guards screamed their threats more loudly, and our cell received an increasing amount of abuse and invective. Handcuffs were displayed more frequently, and the eerie sound of chained prisoners became more prevalent. My cellmates grew tense as the days dragged on. It was apparent that all this was a show for my benefit, and I was only sorry that others had to be affected by it. Nevertheless, the increased hostility and abuse further confirmed the fact that the communists wanted only to destroy the Chinese people. They were making a great effort to intimidate one man, whose confession would contribute to that purpose, with no concern for the others affected by these measures; even the progressives, who had begun to cooperate with them. I felt that capitulation on my part would do the Chinese people great harm. My disgust for the sadistic hypocrisy of the communists grew greater. The increased torment for my cellmates was unavoidable, although extremely regrettable. But there was no reason to believe that these pressures would be reduced even if I did confess.

In fact, the communists themselves seemed to tire of the campaign, and eventually life reverted to its trivial, day-to-day routine. The authorities ignored me once more, evidently in the belief that the threats they had made would become productive when my will was weakened sufficiently by further dehumanization. This is a judgment in retrospect, of course, because at the time the communists took extreme caution to disguise their tactics. At that period they were interested primarily in keeping me in a state of continual doubt and fear.

Then, on July 21, after four days without questioning, the guards ordered me to gather my possessions. I was to leave the prison. This was one month and six days after I had been arrested, and a multitude of thoughts flew through my head in the few minutes required to gather up my ragged clothes and to wrap them in my blanket.

Were the communists so fed up with me that they intended to release me? Hardly, but hope is a persistent emotion. Was I going to a worse prison, to more torture—maybe execution?

The questions became more insistent when, upon leaving, I overheard the guard saying in Chinese that my number would not be needed, because I would not be returning to this prison. Thinking back on the episode, I realized that this idle comment, too, must have been part of the plan, for the authorities knew that I understood Chinese. Naturally I was worried, but I walked from the prison with as much dignity as possible; even though my shoes nearly fell off, because the soles had rotted, and I had lost so much weight that my pants were more difficult than ever to keep at more than half mast.

The formality of permanent departure was observed scrupulously. At the prison office I was handed the possessions that had been confiscated when I first arrived and told to check them. Carefully, I inspected the watch, rosary, eyeglasses, breviary and two hundred Chinese dollars, worth about one cent in American money. When I nodded approval, these items were all taken back, wrapped up again in a handkerchief and handed to the guard.

After making sure no one was in the courtyard or watching from the street, the guard hurried me to a jeep. I was pushed into the back seat between two burly soldiers and told to keep my head lowered so I could not be recognized. Obedience was easy, but the precaution seemed unnecessary. It was difficult to believe that anyone would identify this ragged character behind a five-week beard, which bloomed in four shades of blond and red.

We drove slowly in light traffic through the city I had come to love. Even though my head was bowed, I could see many familiar landmarks, and nostalgia was strong. Periodically, the driver stopped to let other cars cross, a practice favored by few Chinese. This made me doubly suspicious, and I could only conclude that the authorities were taking extra precautions to make sure no one came close enough to see me. If anything, this made me more apprehensive, for it seemed to mean that I was going to disappear for a prolonged period. Under what conditions?

At last we reached the old Chinese City in the southern part of Shanghai, and I was deposited in the South City jail, a crumbling relic customarily used for Chinese prisoners. Instead of any immediate brutality, however, I was treated casually by the guards who registered me. Then I was taken to a cell, and my puzzlement increased. I had more space than before, although that was not saying much, and the normal prison routine was no worse. Unless I was to receive different treatment, why transfer me at all?

One answer soon became apparent. The evenings, in my cell at least, were devoted to another type of brainwashing— the "discussion group." For two hours each night the five other prisoners would talk lustily about political affairs, prodded by a hard-faced youth of about twenty-one, who appeared to be the leader. He started each discussion with praise of the communist regime. Others would chime in, each apparently trying to outdo his fellows in the fervor of his comments. This went on *ad nauseam*, and frequently the prisoners repeated themselves as often and as tiresomely as my interrogators had done. Apparently the authorities had some idea that the mixture of threats and indignities had reached the point where I might be pushed toward cooperation by the effects of this kind of indoctrination. If so, the experiment quickly blew up.

At first I remained silent during these sessions, allowing the Chinese to lie to each other about how much they loved the state and the Party and how relieved they felt after confessing their crimes. When prodded to join in the conversation, however, I soon found a suitable opportunity to refute Marxist dogma and to attack some of the most blatant falsehoods of communist practice.

The leader swiftly jumped in with a bitter attack on the

Church and particularly against Father Bede Chang. This Chinese priest, who held a doctorate in literature from the Sorbonne in Paris, had been on the faculty and board of trustees of Aurora University, in addition to holding other positions. He was by far the most influential teacher, lecturer and writer in Catholic cultural circles. When arrested in 1951 he had gone to jail with his usual jauntiness and confidence. Three months later a friend was called to identify his gnarled, emaciated body. The communists insisted that Father Chang had died of meningitis, but refused to allow an autopsy.

When my cellmate began condemning this priest, I defended him just as vociferously. Then I recounted in detail how Father Chang had been murdered, and shouted as loudly as possible that the Church and everyone connected with it were being persecuted. The "discussion" quickly exploded into a yelling match. The guard promptly opened the peephole, called the young progressive over and demanded an explanation. Of course, the communist youth blamed everything on the "reactionary imperialist."

The guard then summoned me and snarled—with the same slogan-epithets—that I had to obey the rules for the discussion. The purpose, he explained loudly, was to benefit the prisoner by helping him realize his errors and prepare him for a full confession. He yelled like the Mole and looked like the Horse. At this point I also was in full voice. I told him what I thought of the communists and their confessions and their hypocritical persecutions of men like Father Chang.

This fishwifely exchange attracted the attention of one of the interrogators, who had been roaming around the cellblock. He promptly ended the argument by ordering me to sit down and by sending the guard away. The next morning the discussion leader was removed from the cell, and so was the argumentative guard. This was, I suppose, the continuation of the "rotting away" treatment. I was supposed to feel that I was not worth questioning.

The discussion group ceased to function in our cell for several months, but two hours of conversation were still permitted each night. My cellmates were so far advanced toward complete capitulation that they could talk in little more than slogans, and I made no attempt to discuss politics.

By comparison, my stay at South City jail was a rather refreshing vacation. The guards maintained vicious dehumanization, lest the progressives backslide and revert toward being human. But, in general, the routine was somewhat more lenient and the nightly conversations restored some measure of normality, even though I usually remained aloof from them. Contrary to the communist plan, I found great relief and even pleasure in being ignored completely by the authorities, particularly after the series of threatening sessions I had undergone in Loukawei.

This lasted for seven months. One evening I was unceremoniously hauled out of the cell, with all my disintegrating belongings. Without a word, the guard marched me through the echoing corridors and down wet, slippery stone steps to the dungeon. While I shivered in the heavy darkness—for it was now winter—the guard unlocked a thick, heavily barred door and creaked it open. He motioned me into the cell and shut the door quickly. Long afterward I remembered the way his departing lantern was swallowed by the blackness.

I turned around in the tiny cell and realized I was in solitary confinement. Oh, God, I thought, how long? Give me strength! The cold penetrated my bones, and the dampness was like a fog. I had only my summer matting and a thin blanket. My shoes had almost completely fallen apart, and I had no socks. I wore summer-weight tattered trousers and a ragged cotton shirt.

Somewhere outside the cell the raw wind whined, and a shutter banged methodically—like a prisoner pounding the bars. The wind never stopped, and neither did the shutter. Sleep was impossible. So I made a litany of prayers and throughout the night I prayed in time with the banging of the shutter.

The next morning, tired and still apprehensive, I was taken to the prison office. There I was told I was going back to Loukawei, the prison I supposedly had left permanently. After the dungeon, this was welcome news. The homecoming was made more welcome because the communist authorities allowed me to keep a package from my church, containing a thick Chinese quilt and a padded Chinese gown, the warmest possible clothes for the cruel Shanghai winter. I was also given about five dollars' worth of Chinese currency, and was allowed to buy such luxuries as toothpaste and soap.

Caught between this gesture and the emotions created by the dungeon, I was summoned at once before an interrogator. It was clear that he expected me to recognize the symbolism of these two extremes of treatment and to decide my future behavior accordingly. But, frightened and unsure as I had been, I went before him determined not only to avoid capitulation but to maintain absolute silence throughout questioning. I was positive that this was my surest defense and my only complete protection against entrapment.

When the interrogator found out that I would say absolutely nothing, he nearly exploded. "Se ti!" he snarled, his face choleric. The phrase cracked like a curse; and indeed it was, for it literally means: "We are enemies until death."

For this insolence I was made to stand at attention without moving for many hours at a stretch, four or five days a week— for the next eight months. In all, I estimate I spent some six hundred hours in upright stiffness, most of the time listening to endless harangues from the interrogators. I happily wore out between thirty and forty of my tormentors—I finally lost count—but I did not open my mouth.

On each occasion I was summoned to the same interrogation room and, when the judge learned I had not changed my attitude, the long harangue would begin. By this time I regularly wore my long, flapping Chinese gown, and it covered me so completely that occasionally I could bend my knees slightly or move my feet apart. The guards were supposed to make sure that I did not move, but most of them did not care. They stared out the window, smoked cigarettes, yawned; then, periodically, came over and kicked my feet together, beneath the gown.

The interrogators themselves made no attempt to make their lectures interesting or to depart from the broken-record monotony of pat phrases and bromidic slogans. They worked in teams, with one man spelling an exhausted companion, and the singsong rhetoric never ended. Sometimes they would spend the entire day developing the single point that I would never leave the prison if I did not confess. They warned me, at great length, that my health would break down if I remained in jail for any length of time. The authorities had no responsibility for my fate, they said repeatedly, because I was inviting the worst with my stubbornness. Finally, over and over again, they asked whether I wanted to go home and see my mother. She was still living, then, and in her eighties.

The constant repetition of sentence after dead sentence was deliberate. By the hypnotic sameness of their harangues they hoped eventually to break down my resistance through the sheer frustration of listening to them. One moment of irritation on my part, or one instant of doubt that continued stubbornness was worthwhile, might be enough to crack the façade. In time, the monotonous voices, the leering faces, the senseless, hypocritical phrases became a new kind of subtle torture. Although I tried to escape through reverie, it became necessary to keep hold of myself, even in silence.

When this process became too boring even for the communists, who are not easily bored, they would put me in the prison basement, with my nose against the wall. I would be left to stand alone all day, always with a soldier to guard me, to make sure I did not move. Fortunately, the authorities never knew that this was a welcome relief from their singsong monologues, and I began to look forward to this treatment. The task of standing at attention was arduous, but I became adjusted to it and eventually was able to talk myself into believing that it was little worse than sitting all day on the floor.

Perhaps this behavior was childish. But the entire prison routine was a diabolical sort of childishness, and I knew of no better way to combat it than by behaving like a stubborn child.

The communists wanted only one thing—an admission that would lead toward complete capitulation. It was clear by then that the first slip or the first move toward cooperation on my part would only produce increased pressure to force me into the next step. Conversely, I found that each moment of resistance made it easier to resist the next time.

Then a brace of new interrogators began to threaten me more violently, with indirect but ominous warnings. The phrase, "we have ways to make you talk," became part of their routine, repeated endlessly in violent anger—or simulated anger.

One of this team, a barrel-chested man with a shaved head and the manner of a general, would strut before me and shout: "Wait until the next time! Don't think that standing at attention is all you will get. Next time it will be much more severe."

He liked to pace in front of me, as if reviewing troops. "We have just been playing with you until now, because we want to be humane," he would repeat hour after hour. "We can make people talk, but we are humane and dislike using these methods. You are forcing us to do so by your stubborn, capitalistic attitude."

Then he developed a new theme. Time and again, with a slight sneer on his face, he snarled, "We are going to hit you and make you ring just like a gong."

At each summons to the interrogation room, I had to fight the shakiness in my knees and, despite myself, I could not avoid looking at the bare electric wires that protruded from a rough hole in the wall. Would they be used for shock treatment? But the more violently the interrogators threatened the stronger became my determination to resist. The threats themselves placed the communists on the defensive, in my mind, for they proved that neither ideology nor brainwashing was sufficient, without force.

In this mood of uncertainty and stubbornness I was called out of the cell unusually early one morning. Gulping down the last of several bowls of watered rice, I hurried after the guard, hoisting the gown like a skirt to keep up with him. A new interrogator met me, a suave, smooth-talking man, about thirty years old, dressed in the plain khaki uniform of the People's Liberation Army. It was evident he intended trying politeness on me, but his mood changed immediately when I continued to remain silent after my plea of "not guilty."

Then, seated at the table, he launched into a fresh tirade, in which the tones were different but the words unchanged. After about twenty minutes of nonstop rhetoric, I began to ache. A few minutes later the pain in my lower back forced me to interrupt his speech and request permission to go to the bathroom.

The judge jumped as if he had sat on a hot ember. He fumed and told me brusquely that I was a worm for interrupting him so arrogantly. Suddenly he caught hold of a new idea, and his face brightened.

"Certainly," he said, almost pleasantly. "Just write out

your request and sign it." He pushed paper and pen toward me.

"That is against prison rules," I answered. "The state has given us that privilege, and we are not supposed to make a written request. And I do not intend to break the rules."

Then I retreated into silence. For the fifteen months of my imprisonment I obstinately had refused to write anything or sign anything, and this was a sore point with the communists. Every captive was supposed to write both his life history and his confession in his own hand. Now the interrogator apparently thought he would win a psychological victory if he could get me to write anything at all, even such a fundamental request. This was another move in the patient, subtle art of brainwashing.

At my refusal, the judge resumed his tirade for another twenty minutes or more, while the pain in my back grew sharper. Then, with a final bit of bombast, he left the room, ordering the guard to keep me at attention.

For a few minutes the guard and I stared silently at each other. He was a rather simple peasant boy, with a broad face that perpetually looked as tired of the lectures as I felt. Finally, for the record, I asked him for a chance to go to the washroom, knowing that he could do nothing without the judge's approval. The guard shrugged and told me I could be accommodated if I obeyed the judge. "If he wants you to sign a request, sign it," the soldier said.

"No," I answered.

When the interrogator came back and sat down briskly again, he said, "Well, I hope you have had time to reconsider." He pointed to the pen.

I shook my head. At that, he leaned forward and, pointing a blunt finger at me, started scolding again. While he became more and more agitated, the pain became increasingly severe and, finally, there was only one thing to do. I didn't know when I would ever get my clothing washed, but the relief was worth it. I was calm as the judge droned on. From the puddle at my feet, I watched a rivulet slope toward the wall, along the tilted floor. I had drunk a lot of water, I mused.

"When I am speaking," the interrogator shouted, darting around the table and shaking his finger in front of my nose, "look at me."

So I did. I looked him straight in the eye as he kept on yelling, and I saw his expression change from anger to wonderment. Then he looked down at his feet. His cloth shoes had absorbed the puddle. For a moment he stood there dumfounded, then he literally spat out the words: "That proves you're a spy. You learned that in spy school."

Despite myself, I laughed in his face. Stamping his feet, the interrogator returned to the desk. Finally, after comparing me unfavorably to a dog, he dismissed me in disgust. That was the last I ever saw of that particular judge.

A new team took over, and for several weeks they made increasingly bombastic threats. Then, early one morning, two soldiers with drawn pistols came into the cell, one of them dangling a pair of ancient handcuffs. In the interrogation room three judges were waiting. Without preamble, the chief informed me that I had exactly three minutes to talk, and, if I still refused, they would not be responsible for the consequences.

"Two minutes left," the judge said, looking at his watch. "A minute and a half," he counted. "One minute. Thirty seconds."

I stood there, trembling.

The judge roared something unintelligible. The two soldiers grabbed me roughly and quickly handcuffed my arms behind my back. A light gunny sack was thrown over my head, and I was led down the stairs and into the courtyard. I could see through the coarse fabric, which evidently was intended to prevent anyone from recognizing me, and I noticed that the soldiers moved with unusual swiftness. They ordered me into a jeep, and I was flanked by two armed guards. We rolled out into the city.

Once again uncertainty became more powerful than threat. This time the authorities had made no pretense about formally checking me out of the prison. Instead, I had been bundled off without a chance to take my clothes or other possessions. What that meant I did not know—but I prayed fervently.

We drove slowly across the entire span of Shanghai, from the southwest corner to the northeast. The jeep stopped in front of the tall iron gates of Ward Road jail, in the former British concession; the jail made infamous by the Japanese mistreatment of foreigners confined there during World War II. The gates creaked open, and we rolled into a courtyard surrounded by several tall, barred buildings.

At the tallest of these, a frowning eight-story building, a guard prodded me with his gun barrel. I clambered out and the soldiers quickly marched me into the building and up to the second floor. Twice, solid iron doors opened for us. Then, at the end of a long, echoing corridor, I was shoved into a padded cell. The guards hurriedly removed my handcuffs and left, as if afraid of ghosts.

I stood there, uncertain, still shocked and, I suppose, subconsciously thankful that no firing squad was in the cell with me. I was alone for the first time during imprisonment, save for the one night in the dungeon, but it soon became a particularly horrible loneliness. This had been the end of the road for more than one poor victim of the communists.

The octagonal cell was about six feet across and some fifteen feet high. The floor was a leather mat, and leather mattresses covered the walls to a height of about ten feet. Except for a small peephole in the door, there was no ventilation whatsoever. There were no sanitary facilities, not even a bucket; only a corner. Everything was covered with thick, black soot.

Then I saw the mad scribblings on the wall, the legacy of previous occupants. "Down with Mao!" said crude characters scratched in the leather with fingernails or bamboo slivers from chopsticks. "The North Koreans did invade South Korea!" Final rebuttal, final defiance from tortured minds. What happened to these men?

All day I fought off the enveloping depression of this place. I prayed for the souls of those who had been here before me. I went back to the beaches and the football fields of California. I rekindled my defiance of the communists.

That night I heard Wu for the first time. That was the name I gave him, for long ago he had lost his name, as he had lost all else that was precious. Wu lived in another padded cell, five feet away. He introduced himself with a long, piercing wail. Silence—then another wild scream. Tensely I listened, for this was a distraction I had not steeled myself to ignore.

Boom—boom! came the crash of a heavy wooden beam from Wu's cell. It was on a fulcrum, and he was seesawing back and forth. The floor beneath me jumped and throbbed. At each bang of the heavy timber, Wu wailed. Then he struck up a rhythmic beat and, in time with it, began chanting: "Dirty capitalist! Bloodsucking capitalist!" Boom—boom! "Why don't you confess?" He went on for hours, a broken man, driven by fear and implanted hatred into this one instinctive act. "Oh, if I had only confessed," he moaned, "I wouldn't be here now. If I had only confessed I wouldn't be here now."

Wu kept up this ghoulish litany all that night, never missing a beat, never tempering his maniacal screams. Finally, at dawn, he quit with a strangled cry.

For more than an hour my nerves remained knotted, and I could not even lie still. When, at last, I was able to relax enough to think of sleep, the guard banged the door with his club, and my nerves tightened again. All day the guards made sure that I did not rest, while Wu slept. That night, around nine o'clock, he started again, with the same boom —boom and the same accusing cries. He quit at dawn.

On the second day I saw him. My peephole was open when the guards swung back Wu's door to give him food. Instantly an emaciated little man darted into the corridor, rushed over and spit at my peephole. "Capitalist dog!" he yelled. "Capitalist dog!" His eyes were wide and rolling with frenzy. He raised a scrawny clenched fist, as if to bang the door, then the guards carried him back, still screaming, into his cell.

This went on for twenty-five days. Wu started his seesaw regularly each evening and usually continued throughout the night. At every chance during the day he tried to get at me, and once he threw a can of rice at the little peephole in my door. The poor man had been driven mad by communist torture, and now he was their creature.

For more than three weeks the authorities left me alone with Wu and the prowling guards. Rest was virtually impossible, and I drew on all my reserve strength. During this period I had no change of clothing, no bath; not even water to wash my face.

A new interrogator summoned me and began another interminable lecture. Evidently he believed that the demented Wu would soften me into cooperation. When I persisted in remaining uncooperative and uncommunicative, the judge lectured me a few days more, then sent me back to Loukawei, the first prison.

I had won again, and this was a signal victory. After surviving the poor maniac, I knew that I could resist almost anything and so, perhaps, did the authorities. For the remainder of my imprisonment, they maintained the constant pressure of force and threatened force against me but no direct torture was used.

I can only conclude that higher authorities had decided from the beginning not to subject me to physical violence and my stubbornness convinced them later that this would be self-defeating. Perhaps my defiance brought me harsher treatment, but I am convinced that, even if I had confessed, this would not have changed the disposition of my case. As it was, my total sentence was shorter than those of other foreigners who were more cooperative.

The communists killed many Chinese priests when they refused to be used as a front for subverting the Church. But they could not employ me, a foreigner, for this purpose. Instead, like all foreigners, my potential value to them was only to supply a confession that would have made good propaganda and to confuse and subvert my Chinese friends and perhaps those at home in the United States. The authorities, therefore, sought to obtain this confession by intimidation and trickery; not by killing me. Throughout my imprisonment, they seemed confident that eventually I would capitulate to their brainwashing.

Their next tactic was a patient and continual attempt to trap me into cooperation.

Chapter six

ENTRAPMENT THROUGH MINUTE DETAIL

COMMON MISERY USUALLY UNITES MEN and, frequently, brings out many of their finest qualities. The pressure of a shared emergency or a universal hatred generally arouses a basic instinct of group preservation. This is true in war. It is often true in prison, even among hardened criminals. Normally, it is the behavior pattern for prison camps and political prisoners but not among those controlled by the People's Democratic Republic.

Instead, the Chinese communists have developed methods to nullify this instinct and to destroy any group solidarity hostile to them. This was necessary on both a national and a prison level, for Peking intended to control vast numbers of people with a minimum use of communist manpower. Early in their regime the authorities used brainwashing to create unnatural enmities and suspicions among men more disposed to unite against a common foe. The abnormal results were demonstrated by the fact that the released American prisoners came home from Korea as "lone wolves," who avoided contact, for the most part, with anyone who had been imprisoned with them.

At the outset of imprisonment, the prompt and thorough application of "dehumanization" is designed to forestall group solidarity, in addition to destroying the individual. The rules of silence, all the petty regulations governing eating and bathing and, finally, the strong injunction against helping a fellow prisoner are part of this scheme. Men who are disgusted with themselves and their personal appearance can become more easily disgusted with their companions. Denied normal intercourse, most prisoners tend to recede into themselves and, as apathy grows, group consciousness dies.

The communist state moves quickly into this void, as a replacement for lost human contacts; the new symbol of a guiding influence. Moreover, the state attempts at the outset to convince every prisoner that it is not only all-wise and all-powerful but all-seeing, so that everything the captive does and much of what he thinks presumably is known instantly "upstairs." Each cell, therefore, is packed with unidentified, unnumbered informers. Their purpose is to collect information, to pass on warnings from the authoritities, to establish contacts for them and, finally, to trap the unwary into admissions or revelations that can be brought out later, with damaging effect, during interrogation by the judges.

In many ways the prisoner's task of protecting himself from these agents is as wearing as the resistance against overt intimidation. It requires constant wariness, without a moment's relaxation. A verbal slip to an apparently friendly prisoner can be as dangerous as a direct admission, for inevitably it will reach an interrogator. He will exploit it immediately.

I was reminded of this one day by a fellow prisoner who slept next to me for a brief period. He struck up frequent whispered conversations when the guard was absent or seemed inclined to waive temporarily the rules of silence. The prisoner, a wizened little man, told me of another captive who had been put in handcuffs for a period of weeks and cut to half rations because he had given a bar of soap to a cellmate. This violation of a strict rule had happened nearly a year before, and I was the man befriended. The incident occurred when I first arrived in prison, without soap, and I still remembered the gratitude I felt toward my benefactor.

Now the story was being told to me, no doubt, in order to test my reactions, to show me that Big Brother knows all, and, perhaps, to trap me into a damaging statement. I was convinced that little happened by accident in prison and certainly no conversation of this type was spontaneous. The little man who recounted the story probably had no idea that I had been involved. He merely repeated what the judge had told him to say to me, then reported back that I received the news silently and without changing expression.

Any other reaction on my part could have been dangerous to me and, perhaps, to my benefactor. It was quite possible that the authorities did not know for sure who had given me the soap, which a guard discovered. They might have been trying to get me to identify the culprit or to confirm their vague suspicions by my reaction to the little man's gossip. If I had expressed sympathy or, worse, if I had condemned the authorities for this reported punishment, the judge would have a new charge to turn against me on my next visit. In either case, a normal human reaction was to be avoided, for the protection of all concerned. Even the timing appeared to have a purpose. By waiting a year, the authorities evidently expected my memory of the episode to be hazy, thereby throwing me off guard.

From these tiny beginnings the web of spying grew and wound around every one of the several thousand men then confined in Shanghai's jails. The informers usually were weak men who already had slipped into the mainstream of brainwashing and were working with concentrated guile to free themselves from prison through cooperation. Outwardly they often were indistinguishable from the rest of us. Their most noticeable trademark, if they had one, was an initial air of friendliness and affability and a manner of confidential comradeship. Therefore, prisoners with experience automatically shied away from any friendly face; and, if nothing else, this further helped to destroy a group feeling and to increase mutual suspicion.

The authorities sent a veritable regiment of agents of all types into action against me, despite the fact that I had displayed unusual truculence and uncooperativeness during my interrogation sessions. This consistent use of these methods indicated their doctrinaire belief that brainwashing ultimately will work on everyone. It was clear that the communists expected subversion and intimidation to succeed in my case, as they had on more amenable victims.

Naturally, the men whom I identified or suspected as being informers were not always clever, and neither were the authorities. But they were thorough, persistent and constantly dangerous.

One approach, of course, was through my religion. The communists knew I had been informed that an Irish priest had baptized at least two of his cellmates while imprisoned in 1952. Therefore, I was suspicious, but not surprised, when a man eventually showed up in my cell with the claim that he was one of these converts. He knew his Catholic doctrine perfectly. In fact, he taught me the English version of some prayers which I had been accustomed to saying in Chinese.

The precise English wording had faded in my memory. This well-educated man told me he was imprisoned because he had been the Shanghai representative for an airline which ferried C-47 transport planes from San Francisco to the Chinese Nationalist Air Force.

He was convincing and pleasant, and it was a temptation to try rising above the pigsty by talking to him. But I noticed that the guard, watching us through the peephole, made no effort to interfere whenever my friend began a conversation in violation of the rules. This convinced me that my companion was an informer, and the guard was being lenient to let him practice his profession. Needless to say, the effort failed, and the prisoner soon was transferred.

Long afterward I wondered whether my cellmate had been one of the Irish priest's converts or whether he had made a special study of doctrine as a means of deceiving me into cooperation. Weeks later this unresolved question was given a new twist. One day I glanced up from my place on the cell floor, to see a trusty standing outside the window cleaning the bars, this being a jail without the wooden planks of Loukawei. The prisoner slyly nodded a greeting, and I recognized the ex-airline representative. When the others in the cell were not looking, he solemnly crossed himself. Was this done sincerely or as a further part of masquerade? Such suspicions, perhaps, were unpriestly, but they were realistic and fully symbolized my mental attitude at that time.

Next, the communists tried to exploit my interest in physical fitness. The authorities knew the characteristics and habits of their prisoners in considerable detail, so they knew my desire for physical exercise. During the infrequent periods when we were allowed to exercise in our cells, I experienced my only enjoyment while in prison. I spent these fifteen-minute periods in refreshing push-ups, deep knee bends, torso twists and similar drills.

Soon, a miniature Charles Atlas came into our cell, a man with a well-kept, perfectly proportioned body. He joined me in my exercises, and I admired his perfect timing and his stamina. Here, indeed, was an entree for further confidence, which the communist authorities undoubtedly intended. But the muscle man was bird-brained and a boor, and he finally provoked me into several arguments. He quickly disappeared, and I never saw him again.

The authorities waited six months before trying this approach again; when they did, they sent a man of many doubtful talents. About thirty years old, he also was a perfect physical specimen, muscular but lean. With sympathetic friendliness, he struck up a conversation soon after arrival, and went out of his way to compliment me on my spirit. He identified himself as a law professor. While applauding the state's new military power, he insisted the communists were wrong in failing to apply the Anglo-American system of law to New China. He believed in Western law, he said, because of the influence of the American professors under whom he had studied. Needless to say, he did not explain how he thought a dictatorship could adopt a legal system based upon respect for human rights.

Nevertheless, the professor was a stimulant, at a period when I was revolting rather strongly within myself against the accumulated degradation of the prison. He was interested in both muscles and mind, a rare combination in that environment, and he liked to discuss such subjects as the development of Roman Law. In this respect, his characterization was persuasive.

But the professor automatically had aroused my suspicions by arriving in the cell with a large bundle of clean clothing; a status symbol of considerable importance under the circumstances. Later, he was permitted to receive money once a month from his family, to buy toilet articles and vitamin pills. He claimed to have been in prison for more than a year, but he showed none of the normal effects. Furthermore, the guards paid no attention to his violation of the no-talking rule. Nor was he reluctant to voice sentiments in Chinese which were critical of the communists and normally sufficient for prompt official retaliation.

The professor was rather fastidious, and it seemed normal for him to offer to share his soap on the occasions—once every four weeks or so—when we were permitted to wash our clothes. I refused the offer, remembering my previous experience, but noted the gesture as part of the character portrait he was painting of himself. He wore his hair long, explaining that he expected to be released soon, and wanted to avoid having his head shaved, so his friends would not know he had been in prison. Meanwhile, he insisted many times that he had been unjustly imprisoned and intended to resist the communists until the end.

This characterization lasted for several months. Then the professor was called more frequently to the interrogation room, and the session lasted longer on each occasion. This went on for about a month. Usually, he returned full of frankly expressed anger and hostility toward the communist judges.

Finally, the professor began to show signs of tremendous strain and worry instead of the perfect calmness he once had assumed in proclaiming his resistance to communism. Several times he returned to the cell in extreme agitation, after several hours' interrogation. In one of these moods, he grabbed my arm while the guard was away and whispered, "I have a great problem to solve. Father, I need your advice desperately."

This was a moment I always dreaded. A priest's normal reaction, of course, is to give the solace and help that he can. But even that fundamental impulse had to be constantly checkreined, on behalf of the larger number of people who would be affected if I showed any exploitable weakness to the communist authorities. If I had been foolish enough to offer advice to the lawyer, or to any of the dozens of other men who solicited help, the communists would have had an excuse to say that I was meddling in political affairs. Because the charge would have been true, to a certain extent, there was always the possibility that one result would be the beginning of a sense of guilt, if only subconsciously. Despite my defiance, I scrupulously obeyed the prison rules, except when the guards themselves relaxed them in order to avoid this kind of chain reaction; because self-guilt, I recognized, was the foundation of the erosion process. Furthermore, if I had given help to any prisoner who was not working for the authorities, he would have been punished immediately. This would have made guilt almost impossible for me to escape.

So I evaded the lawyer's request, as I had so many others, by simply telling him to follow his conscience and to be true to himself. I found ways even to avoid listening to his problem, to evade another possible trap. This was my inflexible attitude throughout imprisonment, and I never heard of anyone who suffered because of it.

The lawyer seemed distressed and increasingly nervous as his interrogations continued. He spent three or four all-day sessions with the judges, returning in agitated despair to the cell each time. Then one evening he came back radiating peace and joy again. He told me he had confessed to everything and consequently his case had been solved. "My thinking has been straightened out," he said, "and now I realize how foolish all my old thoughts were. I am at peace again."

This was the pat communist-style ending. The authorities never tired of playing out the drama of an agitated, depressed man finding peace again by washing his brain. This performance, of course, was for my benefit, and I was supposed to take the lesson to heart. I was not impressed.

As a special and impressive part of the lawyer's "reeducation," he was permitted to have books again, and he spent considerable time reading. This was a particularly difficult sight for me to resist, for I was starved for reading material. In his contacts with me, the lawyer returned to his pleasantries and frequently talked to me; again, with no interference from the guard.

He usually opened the conversation by asking the English translation of a term encountered in his reading. Since his own knowledge of English was quite extensive, he would try to pin me down to a precise definition. One day he came up with the Chinese expression, "ho hsiang." I popped out with "bonze," the word for a Buddhist priest. The lawyer was not satisfied, and he began pressing me further, with a persistence that first annoyed and then intrigued me by its intended purpose.

The lawyer asked if I was a bonze. When I answered negatively, he then said he had read of Catholics who lived a monastic life, similar to Buddhist bonzes, and wanted to know the term used to describe them. He remained dissatisfied at my reply, that these men were priests or brothers. He insisted there was a specific English term for the inhabitants of monasteries. At that point, after two years' dry rot and skimpy conversations largely in Chinese, I actually couldn't think of the word "monk." This seemed to upset him considerably. He dropped the subject in disgust and returned to his book.

A day or two later the lawyer brought up the same question. Although bored with the topic, I tried again to uncover a suitable word, but failed. Finally, with a slight sneer of triumph, the lawyer himself suggested the word "monk." I laughed and told him his English, at that stage, was better than mine.

I quickly forgot this trivial conversation. Two months

later, however, one of my interrogators revived it. He wanted to question me about a man who had a cousin known by the nickname of Monk. The lawyer's planted questions had been a rather devious way of attempting to trap me into some sort of admission that might implicate me with the man then under suspicion. There was no doubt in my mind that the well-read lawyer was acting as a communist informer. In retrospect, it appeared that my original inability to disinter the word "monk" had stumped him, and he had to wait until he could get further orders from upstairs before actually mentioning it himself.

Once this little task was accomplished, the lawyer abruptly switched to hostility against me. Thereafter, he never spoke pleasantly, but limited his conversation to curses and insults against my religion and my country. I was accustomed to these sudden shifts and was able to shrug off this one. Thinking back on the episode, however, I realize that I must have stifled my emotions rather completely, to accept his long string of insults without permitting them to detonate my Irish temper. If anything, the quick change from pleasantries to hostility exaggerated the impact of the insults, as no doubt was intended.

To a sane person this might sound like nonsense. But it must be remembered that the communist world is not sane and that brainwashing is not a rational process. The communists had demonstrated the infinite patience and subtlety of their approach in this one incident. They demonstrated, moreover, their capacity to capture and misuse a man of considerable intelligence and education. All this waste of time and talent doubtless was considered worthwhile for the minimum purpose of reminding me that the authorities knew a great many details about my past life. If the farce had accomplished its major purpose, I might have revealed a fragment of incriminating evidence or I might have begun to worry myself toward debilitation with some inner anxiety. In any case, the authorities used this type of suggestion in an attempt to jar loose every buried incident of memory, to see if any exploitable weakness lay beneath it.

They already had dulled my senses sufficiently, however, so that the lawyer's prying failed to uncover any emotions useful to them. Perhaps it would have been different if I had felt any guilt or if half-forgotten incidents contained any specific details I was anxious to hide. Consciously, I was able to refrain from giving any information about my friends which I did not want the authorities to learn. But dullness rather than cleverness, I must confess, kept me from falling into the lawyer's "monk" trap and into others of similar nature.

This is much too haphazard to be reliable, however, and I realized later that the prisoner must exercise the same conscious control in such picayunish incidents as when confronted by more overt communist challenges. Since no detail is too small for the communists to ignore or to seek out with this type of indirectness, it follows that adequate defense against brainwashing requires absolute control over even the tiniest particle of memory or emotion. Once again, this is reason for the prisoner to maintain absolute silence, for he can never be completely sure that anything he says will be valueless. I found this far more difficult to do in the cell, however, than in front of the interrogators. This difficulty, I fear, should be recognized in advance.

The lawyer's next gambit was far more transparent and, for me, easier to handle, if no less annoying. His mood of hostility toward me intensified, and I am sure that it corresponded to orders from upstairs. For the four remaining months that he was in my cell, he did everything possible to explode my temper. The purpose quite clearly was to goad me into physically assaulting him, so that the authorities could prove I had shown "contempt" for the Chinese people by striking a fellow prisoner.

Now a merit trusty, the lawyer left the cell twice daily to bring back our so-called food. He always brought either too little or too much rice. If I could not finish the amount given me, the guard invariably cursed me at length for wasting the "blood and sweat" of the people. If there was too little rice, the lawyer, being Chinese, could eat much more quickly than I could, and I would go hungry.

During the exercise period, when we used to coordinate our calisthenics, he now began harassing me. He would bump into me, kick me, and jump in the way when I tried to unkink my legs by walking briskly across the cell. Sometimes he would stick his fists into my face. At times, I had to restrain myself forcibly.

Once, after an infrequent washday, the lawyer made a careful inventory of his unusually large stack of clothing. Then he jumped up and angrily announced that two of his sports shirts were missing—the brand-new shirts which, I noticed, he had brought into the cell with him. With the venom that had crept into his face during the past weeks of real or simulated hostility, he turned to me and stared accusingly.

I shrugged. "If you think I took them, you're crazy," I said. "Where would I put them?" He continued to snort, so I added, "Look, I'll show you." I opened the cloth containing my meager wardrobe of two shirts and two T shirts, plus ragged socks.

This gesture, of course, was fruitless. For several weeks, during every moment of conversation permitted us, the lawyer continued to speculate about the missing shirts. The subject became as repetitiously boring as communist slogans, and it had the same evident purpose of attempting to wear me down. It was obvious that if the shirts, in fact, had been stolen, only the guard could have done so, for our barren cell permitted no camouflage of such evidence. So, by the monotonous repetition of accusations, the lawyer was trying to trap me into making a charge that one of the soldiers was the thief. If I had done so, even in jest or to stifle the tedious conversation, the statement immediately would have become a pretext for the communists to accuse me of slandering the servants of the people, the People's Liberation Army.

In all, I spent six months in double confinement with this man, and I found his harsh obnoxiousness to be one of the most difficult ordeals among all the pressures created by other prisoners. Even the comparative luxury of our relatively uncrowded cell was insufficient to offset his ripping insults and the frustration of holding myself back from any retaliation for them. I was delighted when, in a change of prisons, the lawyer finally was led away; even though I wound up in another filthy cell, overcrowded by eighteen prisoners and myself.

The infinite patience of the authorities in pursuing this method of entrapment, among other tactics, frequently becomes one of the most baffling and incomprehensible aspects of the communist campaign. Impatient Americans are apt to assume that others, like themselves, are anxious to abandon any procedure which does not immediately prove successful. By this theory, events not directly related in time or sequence frequently are regarded as coincidental, instead of as the result of spaced planning. If a particular approach in the first year of imprisonment failed to produce tangible results, the American way would be to use a different method the second year. The Chinese communists, however, employ the same tactic again and again; particularly, it appears through blind adherence to a set formula, but largely in the apparent belief that repetition is the most important aspect of the attack.

In their minds, therefore, brainwashing depends more

upon the cumulative effect than on any sudden breakthrough. Some men may succumb early in imprisonment, and this for the communists is all to the good. But they do not trust even the most convincing convert, for the progressives themselves are subjected to an endless continuation of brainwashing— or reeducation—to ensure the continuity of their capitulation. For those who do not give in so swiftly there are endless variations on the same basic theme which, the authorities believe, will wear down the stoutest opponent, given sufficient time. The prisoner who feels that he has withstood brainwashing by refusing to capitulate during the first few months has yet to encounter the second, third, and fourth waves of attack. He must be as vigilant against these, or perhaps more so, than during the first attempt to manipulate him.

The lawyer, in fact, had conducted the second sustained cellside assault against the recesses of my mind.

Another informer was a thin, wiry peasant from the interior, whose formal education probably had ended around the equivalent of the eighth or ninth grade. But he displayed all the astuteness and shrewdness of a frugal farmer and evidently had learned at first hand all the unscrupulous laws of self-preservation. He had been a soldier with the Chinese Nationalist Army during the long war against the Japanese, or so he said, and by his account he had developed a particular talent familiar in every army.

The soldier had no battle experiences to relate, during his interminable yarn-spinning sessions, but instead was proudest of his record in wheedling food from hapless farmers in the battle area. He carried this talent into prison with him and succeeded in talking the communists into giving him special food rations, because of a supposedly weak stomach which presumably resulted from his strenuous wartime foraging operations. This special treatment itself was a sign that he

126

had turned progressive and was cooperating with the authorities.

Nevertheless, he was a lonely, pathetic man, and I finally yielded to his constant importunities to talk. I settled on my favorite astringent subject of Chinese characters, but the soldier quickly turned the conversations toward the subject of astronomy.

At first I found this acceptable, because it gave me an opportunity to practice my Chinese and it was a comparatively safe subject in which I had some knowledge, having once taught a bit of meteorology to U.S. army students during World War II.

After exploring the rudimentary areas of the earth's movement around the sun, the names of the planets and similar subjects, my material was exhausted, however, and so was my interest. But not so the soldier. With apparently unflagging curiosity, he continued to press constantly for more and more details about astronomy. When I would ask him to trace a particularly difficult Chinese character on the dusty floor with his finger, for instance, he would find some way of including astronomy in his answer. The subject became so tiresome that I had to clench my teeth whenever he mentioned it, even though at that moment I would have given much for just a brief glimpse of the stars.

Nearly three years later an interrogator clarified the purpose of this particular performance by suggesting that he wanted to question me at length about an observatory which had been staffed by the Jesuits at Zikawei, near Shanghai. The soldier's task was to make sure that I recalled every detail of this "spy apparatus," so that I could not use forgetfulness to hide information or obscure any personal guilt.

Inevitably, the prison also included the ubiquitous "I can get it for you wholesale" character. This one was a sharp-featured Chinese, who, no doubt, had made a comfortable profit on the outside by playing on the emotions or greed of the customers with whom he did business. He sidled up to me with an air of sympathy for my plight and a plan which he assured me would quickly bring freedom.

The trader explained that he was a friend of the French Bishop in Ning P'o, the town on the South China coast where, incidentally, some of the sharpest Chinese businessmen traditionally were supposed to operate. The Bishop, who was seventy-five years old, had been imprisoned, then released. My cellmate claimed he had helped arrange the release from inside the same prison.

"It was simple," he whispered. "The Bishop and I fixed up stories that matched. When he was called up by the judges, he told his story and, later, I told the same story to the judges. Since our accounts matched and since the Bishop signed a confession, he was released. You see how easy it is?"

I merely nodded, then said I wouldn't do it. "But you are foolish," the man said. "It would be useless for you to die here. You cannot see your face, but it is terribly pale."

"I thought it might be dirty," I chuckled. "After all, I haven't washed for some time."

The trader seemed startled, but not discouraged, by this reaction. Each morning, at that period, the crackle of waxed paper sounded like gunfire in the cellside corridor, so sharp do prison ears become. The paper covered loaves of bread, delivered regularly to adjacent cells, but never to ours.

"You hear that?" my companion asked. "They are getting bread, and they must be foreigners, like yourself. No Chinese eats bread. They also get milk. That's what those little bottles you see outside the cells are for. You can get that kind of food, too."

I shook my head again. The trader looked at me slyly, then said, "Since they are foreigners, they must be priests like yourself. It is foolish for you to deny yourself. You have to think of your health. The others are."

"No," I answered, "I won't do it."

"You will regret it," the trader said sharply. But I never did.

This was a clumsy, wooden approach, but its evident transparency also was not accidental. The trader, who probably merely repeated what the authorities told him to say, was a stock figure brought into the play at what the interrogators considered to be the proper psychological moment. This overture is by no means as easy to resist, against the backdrop used for the occasion, as it might sound at a safe comfortable distance.

I had been dehumanized and brutalized for a considerable period. The communists had succeeded in reducing my existence to the algae level, where a bar of soap, a pan of clean water, the crackle of a bread wrapper measured life and became immensely desirable. My customary food, at that moment, consisted of watery rice covered with a few stunted potatoes, usually so rotten that the worm holes could be seen in them. I was obliged to finish each portion, of course, or be tongue-whipped for betraying the people. Still I was hungry and, despite myself, had begun to wonder how long I could maintain health on such a diet.

In this realm, the affairs of the world and even of my neighborhood church were supposed to recede from daily memory; and, indeed, they can easily do so, unless forcibly held in the conscious mind. The intent was to reduce me to the point where the significance of a confession no longer seemed as important as I had originally considered it to be. What was supposed to be important was the immediate improvement I could make in my own condition and the way other foreigners, in a similar position, had responded to the same circumstances. The trader's job was to remind me of these considerations, and he did this flatly and without subtlety.

This was, of course, a negative use of group influence. The communists had deprived me of the comfort of the group, but still they wanted the group to be decisive in my own evaluation of the need and value of continued resistance. The temporary advantages obtained by my Chinese cell-mates through cooperation had failed to impress me, and perhaps the authorities had only slight expectations that they would. It would be different, however, if I could be convinced that I was the only foreigner holding out and was, therefore, tilting at an abandoned windmill. I suppose the impact would have been far greater if I had been confined with a large number of Americans and had seen the rewards of their capitulation. It is easy to understand the tendency, as exhibited in the Korean prison camps, for an individual to ask himself, "Why should I be the only holdout? It's only a confession, which no one will believe."

It is at such a moment that the inflexible determination to resist at all costs needs conscious and vigorous strengthening. Reward, even petty reward, often is more difficult to resist than brutality, because then the powerful stimulus of hate is absent. The individual is completely alone in these circumstances, and he must remain completely alone; for he cannot win unless he reminds himself that this is one man's battle and the stakes are too great to be yielded for the petty, temporary gain being offered.

In this siege of the mind and the will, no detail is too small or no weapon too unimportant to be used. Some of the anonymous informers who constantly surrounded me appeared, by the results, to be acute observers and rather accomplished judges of character.

Once I made the mistake of showing my distaste for a type of vegetable then being served to us. It was called "ta t'ou ts'ai" and resembled nothing more than chopped-up wood chips. The vegetable was similar to the more familiar Chinese bamboo shoots, but it was absolutely without flavor and was just as tough as pine. My reaction was duly reported upstairs, and we had this vegetable twice a day every day for six weeks —and nothing else.

At every moment within the cell, then, it was necessary to be on guard against uttering a careless word or expressing a damaging sentiment. It was necessary, too, to hold emotions tightly in check against anger, for the deliberately provocative actions of the lawyer were by no means unique. Any assault on a fellow prisoner, or particularly the constantly infuriating guards, would be a punishable offense against the state. So the informer system bulwarked overt intimidation to build up frustrations and create the inevitable fatigue of maintaining a watch on myself throughout every moment of the waking day.

Notably, none of these informers—who dogged me throughout imprisonment—made any attempt to convert me to a positive belief in Marxism-Leninism. Neither did the interrogators. The repetition of dogma was continual, of course, and it was probable that the authorities might have expected some of it to rub off on me. But dogma appeared to be more important as a means of wearing me down, through the sheer length and monotony of the lectures. While proclaiming the superiority of their system, the authorities made it plain that they regarded power as a more persuasive reason for expecting me to capitulate to the system. When the lawyer, for instance, announced his relief and rejuvenation after confession, he emphasized his elation over being free of guilt, not over the stimulation of a newly accepted ideology.

I concluded, therefore, that the authorities never had any serious expectation of indoctrinating me into accepting communism, and developments confirmed that belief.

Nevertheless, I also was subjected to the dogmatic influence of discussion groups which were held regularly in the cells of two of the four jails in which I was kept. I was sent twice to one of these, the South City jail, the second term occurring after my prolonged experience with the threats of violent punishment and the long periods of standing at attention in Loukawei.

The return to South City jail, on this latter occasion, was hardly auspicious for any sudden acceptance of communism's "benevolence" on my part. I was driven across the city, in handcuffs, in the early post-midnight silence, then hurried to a second-floor cage. As the door closed behind me, I was greeted with yelps and curses. This cell was pitch-black, and I stepped on one prisoner after another, while seeking an open space on the floor. The stench was sickening, for, as I later learned, eighteen of us were crowded in a cell about 8 by 17 feet. The only ventilation came from a slit of a window, 2 feet high and some 6 inches wide, on the outside wall.

The guards solemnized my arrival by posting a new set of regulations the first morning. These were far more severe than the previous rules. For one thing, they prohibited all exercise and made immobile floor-sitting the order of the day, from 5 A.M. to 9 P.M. They also virtually eliminated bathing, and only one bath was permitted during the four months I spent there. Finally, the new regulations specified the death sentence for anyone refusing to cooperate with the government by confessing his crimes.

In this setting, my ragged, defeated cellmates conducted a discussion session almost nightly. This was done under official encouragement—actually an order—and was made possible by an almost complete waiver of the rule for silence. The cell was dominated by progressives who were in various stages of progression toward capitulation. The discussions, it seemed, were designed primarily to hasten that process, and therefore were meant for the further erosion of men already "hooked" and not necessarily to obtain fresh conversions. Looking around at these unkempt, pallid captives, I often wondered whether any of them realized how little tangible profit they were getting from their rather pathetic efforts to embrace the state. For this cell of progressives degradation and dehumanization had been intensified rather than reduced. The new severity of the regulations, for instance, might have been intended primarily to penalize me, and other priests who were kept in other cells in the same jail. But this did not nullify the fact that the progressives were affected by them as much as I was.

The Chinese prisoners gave no sign of recognizing this glaring inconsistency as they began the strange tribal ritual of discussion group. Seated around the floor, in the dust-filtered light from a single bulb, they would begin to talk of the state's goodness and their own unworthiness; softly at first and then with more vigor and animation as the spark of self-hypnosis spread among them.

Each man, in time, apparently was compelled to enter the conversation, and usually each sought to exceed his predecessor in fulsomeness of praise for the government and the sharpness of his own self-condemnation. The peculiar sing-song quality of Mandarin and some of its strange grammatical forms gave a special eeriness to these sessions.

"The government provides for us very well," the leader often would say, to stimulate the conversation. In Mandarin, the sentence translated literally is: Government very good, provides or cares for us—in the sense of caring like a father. In many other cases, too, the flat formalism of the verbal expression was enlarged in each mind by the special connotation of the Chinese characters. This gave the stereotyped sentiments a double meaning in Chinese, which usually is lost in translation. Furthermore, the Chinese have an intense

133

desire to belong to society and to conform to it, if only to save face, which made them more responsive to the pressure of discussion groups than the average foreigner might be.

"I am a spy," went one refrain, "I am a spy, and in the old days I would be shot. But now I have a chance to make a new life for myself. The state is good to me."

"I must solve my problem through confession. It is only by confession that my thoughts can be corrected and my case can be solved. Then I can go home."

"I am not worthy. I deserve reform through labor for many years."

And on it went, in a monotonous, ever-heightening singsong. All the pat phrases came out: "li kung," to gain merit; "shen ch'ing," the humble supplication of an inferior to a superior; the all-inclusive "wo men yu hen hao te chi hui yao ch'iu chin pu," the opportunity of a lifetime to seek progress. They talked of "American imperialism" and the need to defend the state from it. They talked of having their brains cleansed of capitalist ideas. They kowtowed verbally to the all-wise, beneficent government.

In this mood it was easy for these men to believe—pretend to believe—that being in a filthy jail was a privilege, not punishment; for it gave them the opportunity to recognize their errors and to undergo reeducation away from them.

The state was giving them a chance to redeem themselves and to become "persons" once more; holding this out as a reward to be earned. It was the state, of course, that had made outcasts of these men, forcing them into deprivation and hardship to regain a minimum position in the arbitrary New Society. Anyone capable of recognizing this cynical irony naturally knew better than to mention it amid the array of communist power constantly in evidence. But it seemed to me that these progressives actually were incapable, at that time, of realizing the subterfuge being practiced on them.

The state had thrown them into such degradation and had intimidated them so completely that any sign of leniency or improvement made them grateful. They no longer hated the state for its original cruelty, but fawned on it because it now seemed less cruel and they expected it to become more benevolent. So they could sit in airless filth, praising the men who kept them there and ignoring the fact that cooperation had not yet brought them improvement. Such is the power of brainwashing.

Just what the authorities expected me to derive from these discussion groups never became completely clear. I doubt if they believed I would succumb to any of the slogans, even in the original Chinese. They probably hoped, however, that the impact of this peculiar form of group pressure would become another influence to wear me down. I was supposed to be in a state of such physical exhaustion and mental intimidation that the authorities might have believed only one additional push was necessary for capitulation. Perhaps they expected me to conclude that I would degenerate eventually into the same state as my self-critical cellmates and that to prevent this I might confess more quickly and "solve my case." Whatever the strategy, it failed to work.

I attempted to remain aloof from these discussion groups as a matter of prudence as well as preference. I did not want to become involved in any situation obliging me to admit that I was a criminal. More importantly, I did not want to be maneuvered into any criticism of the United States, a constant undertone for these sessions. But my cellmates periodically urged me to participate, doubtless under orders, claiming, among other arguments, that otherwise I would show contempt for the Chinese people.

Each session was supposed to begin with a sort of brief "business meeting" on the practical problems of the cell. The most important of these concerned the distribution and use of water, for face-washing and, periodically, for laundry. As the latest resident of the cell, I was getting short rations of water, and I was eager to correct the situation. So, one night, I entered into the business meeting.

My cellmates immediately insisted upon following democratic procedures because, of course, in their condition they believed the state when it told them they were living in a democracy. So I taught them Robert's Rules of Order—how each speaker is recognized in turn by a chairman; how motions are made, seconded, and discussed, and how orderly votes are taken. Seated around the cell, unkempt but eager, the prisoners began to discuss the vital question of how to distribute the supply of water, purposefully kept insufficient by the authorities. Speeches were made and numerous proposals offered. Each suggestion required a motion, a second, discussion, and a vote. This can be a lengthy process.

When the subject had been exhausted, the water problem still had not been solved. But, as self-appointed chairman, I had been able to stretch out the time so completely that the entire two and one-half hour period was gone. There was no chance that evening for wailing self-criticism and its hypnotic propaganda effects. Instead, I had used a democratic procedure to disrupt at least temporarily a communist maneuver, just as communists in many Western countries have employed the same tactic to advance their aims in vulnerable groups. This gave me a moment of supreme satisfaction, for at least I had given these men a glimpse of democracy in action. But when the others realized what I had done, Robert's Rules went out the window and Mao's rules were reinstated.

To avoid the pressure of the group and the traps set by the informers, the prisoner must consciously and deliberately cut himself off from all his fellow inmates. He can never be sufficiently sure of himself or of any cellmate, under conditions such as these, to avoid every chance of making an error that might profit the communist authorities. When I learned the importance of even the smallest incident or scrap of conversation within the cell I maintained constant wariness in every contact with fellow prisoners.

This is not always easy. It requires perpetual vigilance which, by itself, becomes another burden in a fatigued atmosphere. After prolonged interrogation or threats or intimidation there are moments when even the grimy cell becomes a refuge and a man longs for some human comfort, if only from a person he distrusts. This normal instinct can be denied only with the most resolute determination. Yet it was necessary in my circumstances. And, unfortunately, it was necessary in the Korean prison camps. The record shows that the reverse influence of the group, in all the ways I have illustrated, was an important element in pushing many American GIs into cooperation with the communists.

It follows, then, that the true "lone wolf" has the only adequate defense against this influence.

The communists rely so heavily upon this perverted group pressure that they built it into the greatest danger I faced. During one period of my imprisonment I was assigned a place on the cell floor between two obvious agents of the authorities. The allotment of space was planned, of course, and so were the prisoners' tactics.

They were coarse men, both of them. One was a thin, bony merchant, with a cocked eye and a face marked by sly distrust. The second had been fat, although his skin now hung in ugly folds. His soft, flaccid face was marked by dissipation and the erosion of constant opportunism. When I first saw them, they reminded me of the two guards, the Mole and the Horse, who had so plagued my early weeks in jail.

All day these men talked; in loud, harsh and unrefined Chinese. They talked across me, as if I were not there, and I could not escape them, not even by pressing back against the wall. With their faces only a few inches from mine, each man roared into one ear, and their spittle flecked my cheeks when they became excited. The guard made no effort to stop their marathon conversations, and all of my requests for silence were haughtily ignored.

Worst of all was what they said. "The Americans are a bunch of bloody, ruthless imperialists, and they are trying to enslave the Chinese." "The United States wants to plunge the whole world into war, and the peace-loving peoples cannot build the new society until they destroy the United States." "The Catholic Church is the advance agent for imperialism, and it must be destroyed." "This priest here, this bloodsucking capitalist, is a spy and our enemy until death. He will rot in jail." "The priest cannot be reformed, for you can teach nothing to a blockhead and a saboteur."

All day and every day, when I was in the cell, they screamed this same refrain, over and over again. My Irish temper constantly boiled, and I dug holes in my palms with my clenched fists. It would have been suicidal to lash out at them, even verbally, so I remained silent and added another faggot of frustration to the fire within me. It was impossible to concentrate upon escapist thoughts or to meditate or to pray, so booming were these hateful voices. My nerves were coiled like a spring.

When it seemed that I could stand my odious companions no longer I was summoned to the interrogation room and, as intended punishment for insolence, sent to stand at solitary attention in the prison basement. This happened frequently, for this was the time of my prolonged periods of remaining at attention in retaliation for refusal to discuss my case. The authorities obviously believed they were giving me the strongest possible nonviolent punishment. In fact, the insulting conversation that erupted whenever I was in the cell was far worse.

If I had been forced to listen to these two men without relief I think I might have lost my mind. I am sure this was the closest I came to cracking throughout the entire three years. The authorities had proved the importance of group pressure, but they failed to detect its effect on me. I was saved because they believed the group instinct so strong in everyone that solitude was severe punishment. Once again they were defeated by a reaction contrary to their predetermined expectations.

All the various artifices used to trap me within the cell, it turned out, were only a part of communist trickery. There was still more to combat.

Chapter seven

CELL-SIDE ATTEMPT
AT INDOCTRINATION

IN COURTROOMS, THE PURPOSE OF CROSS-examination often is to trap unwary witnesses or prisoners into revealing facts they have forgotten or wish to conceal. Even in the United States questioning and innuendo are accepted tactics, and each year thousands are lured into confusion, inconsistency and revelation. They include the guiltless, as well as the guilty, and many who, no doubt, had resolved firmly beforehand to avoid every trap. The majority of these men and women are well-fed, well-clothed and comforted by the support of friends and relatives. They know that the state will fully protect their rights and that they cannot be forced to testify against themselves. Still, through interrogation alone they can be made to contradict themselves, to doubt their own memories and observations of events; perhaps even to lose self-confidence.

Communist authorities have the same purpose for cross-examining prisoners under their control. But there the similarity ends. The average prisoner—tired, degraded and underfed—is no longer sure of himself. He has no rights and no one to speak for him. A single, unguarded statement, he realizes, can jeopardize his well-being and endanger friends. Fatigue often plays tricks with memory, and his senses have been dulled by long isolation and the monotonous repetition of charges and propaganda. Yet even a misstatement honestly made can be dangerous for him. Finally, punishment and reward have been used with scientific exactitude to destroy his resolve.

The communist prisoner, therefore, must be doubly vigilant against self-incrimination, with only a fraction of normal reserve strength. Moreover, every period of questioning amounts to a trial, whether conducted in a formal court or a dismal room, for its ultimate aim is to produce a confession of crimes or to hasten progress toward one. Each admission makes the next one easier, and each moment of doubt or confusion decreases resistance. It is during these interrogations that the communists attempt to pull together all the strands of cellblock pressures in an effort to bend the prisoner to their will. In turn, the corrosive effect of a mistake during interrogation is expected to eat deeply into the prisoner's resolve, creating worry, fear and guilt, when he is back in his cell and submerged once more in his own thoughts.

The first mistake, then, is usually fatal. For, from initial error, the communist strategy is patiently to lead the captive toward self-revelation, misstatements and contradictions. One purpose is to involve the prisoner so deeply that a further admission becomes inevitable. He then can be jockeyed into revealing so much about himself that the last bit of important information or the final confession seems insignificant. A second motive is to create such a sense of self-guilt and self-doubt that the captive's erosion is accelerated. All this is practiced with patience and subtlety by trained and thoroughly experienced interrogators.

In my case this process began with deceptive obliqueness when I first faced an interrogator.

"What is my crime?" I asked.

"We know, but we want you to tell us," he said, with the affability he assumed at the start of the interview.

"But I have done nothing wrong."

"Then you should not be afraid to talk," the judge said. "You tell us everything and, if you have done nothing wrong, you can go home."

"I've already told you everything," I replied.

"Oh, no," the interrogator answered, "you have not told us everything yet. You must be a criminal or you would not be here. I suppose you do not understand our law, because of your corrupt background. Now, frankly and honestly, tell us everything, and we will explain the meaning of your actions. Only in this way can you and I work together to solve your problem." The interrogator smiled benevolently.

"But I haven't committed any crime."

He shook his head sadly. "You must put aside your reactionary way of looking at things and adopt our progressive point of view. Forget the 'old society' and live in the 'new society.' Then you will see clearly."

"But," I persisted, "I know my point of view is correct."

"No, it is not!" he snapped.

It was after this exchange that I accused him of being the criminal for imprisoning me, got myself ordered to attention —and saved myself a great deal of trouble. For the purpose of this beguiling, deceptive approach was to get me talking. The more I talked, the authorities reasoned, the more deeply I would dig myself into their trap. If I confided in them, or pretended to confide, the first breach would be made in my wall of self-defense. After that, they believed, widening the breach would be only a matter of time and patience. By retreating into stubborn, schoolboy silence I employed the only effective defense against this attack.

The communists easily spot a compulsive talker, and they work on him vigorously. They do the same for the debater, who intends to outwit them, or for the man who expects to defend himself through indifference. When these types talk, they become vulnerable. More than one prisoner, who was determined not to reveal any information, has found himself slyly sidetracked into making statements which proved to be very useful propaganda for the communists.

After orally giving his life history, the prisoner invariably is asked next to write his autobiography, in detail, from the time he was six years old to the present. These requests usually are made with mildness, and the prisoner is led to believe this a mere formality. To heighten this impression, the communists gather a considerable amount of information about each prisoner and delight in telling him obscure facts about himself. The implication is that a written biography would be harmless, because it would merely repeat the details already known to the authorities.

During my jail term, the interrogators revealed a surprising range of knowledge about my affairs. They knew, for instance, that I had made a special study of communism at the University of San Francisco twenty years earlier. They knew that my brother worked for the Federal Bureau of Investigation. They described in detail the financial support for Jesuit mission work in China; facts which I did not know at the time but later substantiated. They reminded me that several years earlier I had collaborated as a translator on an article about communism. This particular event had faded completely from my memory, and I still do not know what languages were involved; although I am sure the communist authorities do. The communists described in detail the secret plans which had been made for the training of seminarians and beginners in religious life, another point I checked and found accurate. They even knew how frequently I myself went to confession.

Often it is extremely disconcerting to sit—or, usually, to stand—in front of a judge and have him describe, with complete accuracy, many of my characteristics and a large number of my likes and dislikes. Food preferences, hobbies, favorite sports and books, and so on. The authorities could tell me that, although ordinarily I am right-handed, I deal cards with my left hand. They not only knew who my special friends were, but they had a complete dossier on even my casual acquaintances, some of whom I had completely forgotten. One day the interrogator showed me a picture of a young Chinese of about twenty-five. The picture itself did not stir up memories, but the judge explained that, eight years earlier, the Chinese had been my Mandarin teacher for about six months. Only after this explanation did I recall the man and realize that, again, the all-seeing state had its facts straight.

"You see," the judge invariably would say, "we know all about you. We are not asking you to tell us anything new. Just write down all the details."

On my first encounter with this approach I had to exert conscious pressure, again, on myself to avoid the trap. The statement sounded plausible enough on the surface. But I suspected—and later proved to myself—that the authorities did not know everything they wanted to know about me and were seeking further details through the device of a written biography. Furthermore, as I also later confirmed, the writing of the individual's life history is by no means as simple as it is made out to be.

The communist purpose is to profit from minute details.

The prisoner who agrees to write out his life story is put into a room by himself and given one sheet of paper at a time. As he completes each page, it is collected by the interrogator or a watching guard, and the captive never sees that page again. On he writes, sometimes as many as several hundred pages, with each completed sheet promptly snatched from him. One prisoner told me that he had written more than two thousand pages of his life history. When the task is finished, the prisoner is told to begin again. Once more he starts from his childhood and wanders down the years. This process may be repeated as many as five or six times.

Then the captive is called before an interrogator, who has been critically examining the various versions of the life story and is ready to explore them. Even professional writers have difficulty in remembering the precise details they have set down in earlier pages of a manuscript, and the amateur is no less troubled. Moreover, the difficulty increases when several accounts of the same events are spread over a period of days. So, inevitably, contradictions and discrepancies occur, along with frequent errors of fact. Painstakingly, over and over again, the judge asks for an explanation of each difference, until he gets what he wants or until the prisoner himself becomes so confused that he only sinks deeper into the morass. In the midst of this process, trick questions or disguised probing can bring out damaging new facts which, when once admitted orally, become easier for the bewildered, tired and frightened prisoner to substantiate in writing.

More seriously, the repetition of written events usually involves friends, relatives, or wartime buddies.

To write so much about oneself without revealing confidences or details incriminating to others is practically and psychologically impossible under the best of circumstances. There is even less chance of avoiding this if the individual has been debilitated by months or years of imprisonment. I have never met anyone who submitted to this process without afterward experiencing extreme regret over some of the things he inadvertently had written about others and which might be harmful to them. Here was a perfect starting point for a massive guilt complex.

Once the prisoner makes the first mistake of talking in any detail to his interrogator he becomes vulnerable to pressures to commit his words to writing, thus starting the whole process. If he refuses to write he feels that all his efforts at reasonable explanation have been wasted. He begins to tell himself that he might as well go on, because he usually is under the delusion that he has given the communists no useful information in his verbal account and will exercise the same discretion in whatever he writes. But this seldom happens.

After my first abbreviated, and unacceptable, oral account of my life history, I receded into silence and provided no further information. Consistently, and sometimes almost daily, I was asked and refused to write any confession or to sign any document that could become incriminatory.

The communists never gave up their attempts, however, to get me to do so. This was the reason, of course, for the long hours of standing at attention, the violent threats and the performance of my friend Wu in the padded cell. It was behind much of the surveillance within my cell, for the authorities hoped to secure evidence with which to trick me or embarrass me into confession.

The authorities also used other methods. Eighteen months after my first and only oral statement, an interrogator read back my brief life history during one session. "All we want you to do," the judge said, calmly and politely, "is to write this out. If you will write out this account of your life, then we will have a document by which we can settle your case." He looked up at me slyly and added, "Our whole purpose is to clear up this case of yours, to get you out of the country

146

and home to your mother as soon as possible."

It was obvious that, once started, I would have been required to keep writing a fuller and fuller biography until the authorities obtained what they wanted. The interrogator in this instance seemed to think that the gambit would succeed, even though I had evaded the same trap repeatedly throughout imprisonment. His confidence emphasized the point that the communists invariably expect to bring a man around to their manipulation, given enough time and enough pressure. He did not seem disturbed by the fact that once more this rather transparent approach had failed. Instead, his attitude was: Well, after you have been softened up a while longer, we will try the same thing again. This was a rather chilling reminder that the communists were not necessarily interested in pitting themselves against a logical, conscious mind; they were just waiting for the time when logic and volition had been dulled sufficiently for them to attack the weakened mind.

On another occasion, my diet suddenly was changed and, instead of thin, watery rice, I was given "mant'ou," Chinese steam bread, to eat. This is heavier than American bread and actually more nourishing. The change was extremely welcome, but by that time I had had enough experience to regard it suspiciously. After a few days of this, I was summoned back to the interrogation room for more questioning and lectures. Again, I refused to discuss my life history.

The judge then almost casually asked me to sign a piece of paper which was called, euphemistically, the court record. Actually, the interrogation between the prisoner and a single inquisitor was identified as a proceeding of the People's Court; even though it was only in a small room and the only others present at any time were a guard and, frequently, a girl stenographer. But this was one of several types of courts before which the average prisoner was taken, and my time to appear in a more formal court was yet to come.

When the judge pointed to the document to be signed, I asked immediately, "Is this court record signed by criminals?" "Of course," the judge replied lazily. "All criminals have to sign before their cases can be finished."

"Well, I am not a criminal and, therefore, I cannot sign the court record." The judge looked up in surprise. "Since I am not a criminal," I continued, "I would be breaking your law by signing, and I do not want to break your law and become a criminal."

"That has nothing . . ."

"Instead," I persisted, "why don't you sign the court record, because of all your crimes against the people and the Church?"

The judge literally leaped out of his chair and, in violent anger, gave me a long, new lecture on all the cruel and harsh punishments the People's Democratic Republic could inflict. Eventually he dismissed me, but I was recalled time and again and ordered to sign. Each refusal set off another long speech. Finally, the interrogator reminded me that I had been given bread for some days now and implied, with customary indirection, that this privilege could be stopped at any time.

This threat was expectable, but it gave me a fresh line of reasoning to mull over on my way back to the cell and during the next few hours of meditation. It was possible, I thought, that I might become so accustomed to the bread that it would become a necessity despite my best efforts. If I showed this slight weakness, even to myself, I would become vulnerable. Therefore, I had to take the initiative to prevent being trapped by my own meager tastes.

At the next meal, that afternoon, I refused to accept the bread from the guard and demanded the same ordinary rice which the other prisoners were eating. The guard looked at me in amazement, pulled the bread back and left the cell shaking his head. This move was unexpected and upsetting to the communists. As I expected, I received no food that afternoon or the next morning, but by the following afternoon I was back on the rice circuit.

Although the food never was palatable, the loss of a full day's ration was sufficient for me to feel the effects. But I learned an extremely important lesson from this incident. I had cut myself off from a possible temptation and, consequently, had become more capable of resisting communist attempts to undermine me by manipulating food. This victory, minute as it might appear, strengthened me immeasurably; for every tiny triumph in jail creates more confidence and resolution, just as every defeat breeds more and more weakness. From this I realized that a negative defense, however effective, was not enough by itself to meet all the various challenges of entrapment. I had to take the offensive, just as I had been obliged to fight off the first effects of dehumanization by launching a religious argument with my guard.

Curiously, my chance to fight back with the only weapons at hand—the use of trifles—came under unexpected circumstances. On one of my innumerable trips to the interrogation room I was asked, surprisingly, to have a chair. A package was on the judge's otherwise plain desk, but he ignored it and launched into his usual lecture. At the end, when I still remained silent, he said casually, "Oh, by the way, here is a package for you."

He handed it to me, and I saw that it had been addressed in my mother's handwriting. The package had been sent from San Francisco to the Chinese Red Cross in Peking and finally forwarded to the prison. I could only guess that it had been on the road a long time.

"Open it," the judge invited.

I found in it, of all things, a three-pound tin of cookies. The package was so unexpected that, momentarily, I was thrown off guard. I agreed to accept the cookies, in the belief that the judge's gesture was sincere. I saw nothing wrong when he asked me to sign a receipt, because I had done this on one or two occasions when clothes were delivered to me from the church. There was nothing incriminating in this.

But when I moved to pick up the package the judge stopped me. "So sorry," he said. "You cannot take the cookies with you. We have to get our doctors to examine them in our scientific laboratory. You see, we must be sure that they do not contain poison or that they have not spoiled on the way here from America." Angry with myself, I stalked out of the room, realizing that the judge intended using the cookies— my own cookies, if you will—as part of his game of reward and punishment. Having accepted them, it was up to me now to nullify this communist strategy or slide backward in my attempt to assume the offensive. It would have been better to refuse the gift in the first place—but the outcome proved beneficial.

For more than two weeks there was no sign of the cookies nor any explanation for their disappearance. At every opportunity, however, I reminded the interrogator that he had made me sign a receipt for something I did not receive. "This only proves," I insisted repeatedly, "your hyprocrisy, your dishonesty and your insincerity." On each occasion the attack caught him without a defense, and because he had lost face, I escaped the retaliation that might have come from a dictatorial jailer who was neither a communist nor a Chinese.

Finally, the judge beamed at me when I came before him and said he had investigated the story of the cookies. "The laboratory found that they are unsafe," he said, "and so, to protect your health, we cannot give them to you. But we will hold them for your release.'

"That is neither a satisfactory nor a convincing explanation," I shot back. "You know very well that tens of thousands of food packages have been sent to China from the

United States and none of them have spoiled. Besides, how can cookies spoil?" The judge wearily sent me back to the cell.

For the next month I kept up this constant refrain whenever I was called for interrogation. I used the incident to revive my charge that the communists were persecuting the Church and that they had imprisoned me only because of my religion, not for any crime. It would be a waste of my time, I said, to talk to a judge guilty of this insincerity. In a few days the judge disappeared from the case.

At the start of my first session with his successor I brought up the cookies again. Although still refusing to talk about my case, I spent considerable time in recounting the tale of the missing package. The judge, nettled and disturbed by the attack, said he knew nothing of the incident but would investigate.

Nothing happened for another ten days. Then the guard opened the cell door, stood momentarily in the doorway and threw the tin of cookies on the floor. The lid flew off, and the cookies crumbled and scattered on the floor.

"Look what you have done!" I shouted. "You are wasting the blood and sweat of the working people of America!"

While the guard stood in silent puzzlement, I sat down on the filthy floor and ostentatiously picked up every crumb I could find, dropping each one back into the tin as deliberately as we were made to pick up every grain of spilled rice.

When the new judge called me back for interrogation, he had received reports of this attitude from the guard and from the cell informers. At first, he ignored the cooky question and proposed that we start my case all over from the beginning. Evidently he expected that, despite my public anger in the cell, I would have a feeling of gratitude toward him.

So he began to smile when, in answer to his proposal, I said, "All right, let's review the whole case—but on one condition."

"What is that?"

"You must admit that the other judge is a liar, for what he told me about the cookies. And I think this ought to be done according to the procedures of the People's Democratic Republic. That means that he should be called to this interrogation room, before you and the guard and me, and should publicly acknowledge his fault in lying about the cookies."

The judge looked at me incredulously, drumming delicate fingers nervously on the table. "Oh, this is only a small incident," he said. "Why not forget it? You have the cookies now. You should be satisfied. I think this whole thing has been a misunderstanding."

"Forget it," I replied, "when I have been victimized? If the other judge is not a liar, than you are insincere. If he was not lying when he said they were spoiled, they must be spoiled and you know it. So you are trying to poison me!"

The drumming increased, while the judge fought for control. Clearly he did not expect to become the target for this old communist trick of twisting words into a trap. He could not admit the charge against his predecessor, a representative of the people's government, who was, therefore, innocent of any accusation by an outcast from society. Neither could the judge admit that he had given spoiled cookies to me, for this would have been a serious loss of face. With his own techniques turned against him, he was helpless. He solved the problem by sending me back to the cell, leaving me there for a prolonged period. For several months afterward, however, I revived the cooky issue at every opportunity, using it to keep my tormentors off guard.

Each move in my campaign was fully planned beforehand, and I carefully rehearsed in my mind the exact phrasing of every sentence. I spent hours memorizing my line of attack and anticipating the parrying of the counterattack I expected from the authorities. This was absolutely necessary. There was an area of communist and Chinese psychology which I could probe relatively vigorously without fearing brutal retaliation, but only if I used the right words and the right issues. In the Case of the Crumbled Cookies, I had put the authorities on the defensive, because they were wrong and because they had openly displayed this error. This was a matter of semantics and behavior, not a matter of principle. As long as I confined my attack to these narrow limits, and used only communist methods of implementing it, I was safe. If I had attempted to go further or if I had shown either weakness or overbearing arrogance, the results could have been catastrophic. At the same time, for my own well-being, I had to withstand any communist attempt at entrapment by turning my words against me.

This became a sort of minuscule military operation. It occupied much of my waking time, and the therapeutic effect was marvelous. My soggy mind came alive in the constant effort to anticipate every communist trick and to prepare against it. I was sharpened against the deviousness of the informers within the cells and forewarned against the trickiest question from interrogators.

Far more than its defensive value, however, this activity gave me both the exhilaration and the release from pressure that could come only from assuming the offensive. While my "fortress of silence" during interrogation periods kept me from making any verbal mistakes, it was, after all, a negative defense. The judges had ample opportunity, and used it, to flood me with the torrent of words that is an important part of the erosive impact of brainwashing. Even while remaining silent, it was a fatiguing effort to avoid anger over their insults and infuriation over their propaganda. By assuming the attack, however, I saved wear and tear on myself and put the interrogators under the temporary strain of confused

defensiveness. No general ever won a more personally grati-
fying victory than my campaign of the cookies.

The subject of religion became my only weapon above
the level of trifles. When the communists made the mistake,
early in my imprisonment, of showing their sensitivity and
defensiveness to the charge of religious persecution, I used
this issue at every possible opportunity. I turned it against
the interrogators with the same ruthless persistence that they
employed in exploiting any weakness shown by a prisoner.
This led to numerous stormy sessions, for I waived my vow
of silence on this one question, and many times I sounded
more like the inquisitor than the victim. Some of my punishment, no doubt, resulted from this obstinate attitude, but in
the end my treatment for being belligerently hostile was
little worse than if I had been completely complacent.

One of these running debates occurred while I was being
kept in the padded cell at Ward Road jail and being enter-
tained by the nightly screeching of poor Wu. The interrogator spent hours trying to prove that he knew the Catholic
Church and, to demonstrate it, quoted extensively from
canon law; far more extensively, I confess, than I could do.
All this, of course, was merely preparation for an eventual
vicious propaganda assault on the Church. When the propaganda began, I returned to silence, and the debate, as such,
was over. After talking to himself for several more long sessions, the judge assumed an air of benevolence and finally
asked me why I would not talk to him.

"It would be a waste of time," I replied. "All of your
theoretical nonsense about the Church has been completely
refuted in China. You communists are merely conducting a
campaign of blind persecution." He looked up sharply, and I
began a long, detailed account of the cases of imprisonment
and torture of Chinese priests, which I knew from firsthand
information.

At last the judge coughed in embarrassment and said, "Well, I really do not know anything about these cases. You see, I just came down here from the north. But you can be sure that I will investigate, to see if your charges are true."

This was a rather curious attitude, under the circumstances, and afterward I puzzled over its meaning. While the judge "investigated," I was undergoing my most excruciating torment: the nightly yowlings of Wu and the frequent glimpses of his tortured face. The judge conceivably could have tried to reduce me to the same blabbing impotence; and I might have feared this, as reprisal for my religious charges, if I had not been so confident that my attack was well within the margin of safety provided by communist psychology. Moreover, the judge had attempted to save his own face over this issue, instead of destroying mine, and this further demonstrated the weakness and vulnerability of the regime on religion.

Nevertheless, Wu had stretched my nerves like taut piano wires before the judge sent for me again. He said nothing of the so-called investigation but, with an air of affability, suggested that I return to my original prison, Loukawei, and discuss the entire question with the interrogator who handled my case there. The prospect of leaving the padded cell and the nightly nightmare was so tempting that, again, I had to hold myself in check.

"I am sure," the judge said mildly, "that this is all a misunderstanding. The questions that you raised can all be explained. So, if you agree to talk about them, I will release you from the padded cell and send you back to Loukawei."

When I hesitated and remained silent, he said, "Well, what do you say?"

"Do you mean that I will be expected to discuss only the question of religious persecution, not my life history?"

"That is right. You have my word on it."

155

"Well, I will think about it," I said. "Give me a few days."
The judge hid his surprise and sent me back to the padded
cell. I received the impression that he wanted to get rid of
me and was taking this opportunity of doing so. If so, the
motive hardly was benevolence or any concern over my welfare under Wu's clamorous ministrations. Unless a deeper
trap was being laid, it was probable that my resistance to the
padded cell treatment had caused him to lose face, because
three weeks of maniacal neighborliness was supposed to break
any man. Rather than admit further failure for this method
of persuasion, the judge might have wanted to see me go
quickly.

I considered these and many other angles carefully during
the next few days, when Wu and the guard gave me time
to think. Finally, I decided that I could defend myself against
any pitfall and told the judge that I would talk, but only
on religious questions. So I went back to Loukawei and
prepared for the grand debate.

The judge at Loukawei ignored the question, as might
have been expected, during the first few sessions after my
return. Instead, he picked up the attempt to talk me into
confession as if there had been no interruption, no padded
cell and no agreement over religious discussion. He spent a
great deal of time, at this point of my post-Wu period, in
trying to convince me that health was endangered by prison
and that I should do something about it; namely, confess and
go home. To prove the point, he gave me long details on
how his own health had been troubling him. He told me repeatedly how his doctor had advised him to give up smoking
his two to three packs of cigarettes a day. Instead, he constantly sucked on hard candies, but this failed to disguise
his nervousness.

The judge, a young fellow in his thirties, was distinguished
only by a constant air of cockiness. A smooth, glib talker, he

seldom allowed any self-doubt to show behind his façade of confidence. He was of medium height and rather slight build, a combination that gave no distinction to his plain army uniform. He became unusual only when he cracked out long and carefully polished sentences of dogma.

The interpreter this time was one of the drab old-young girls created by the communist regime. I nicknamed her Agnes, because I thought she needed something that was feminine. In the bulky army uniform worn by all women at that time she looked like an undernourished recruit; a frail, hesitant nonentity, wearing thick glasses and a squint. Although she appeared to be still in her twenties, she already had become prissy, old-maidish and, it seemed, very unhappy. She attempted to compensate for this by the fervor of her support for the regime and by scrupulous obedience to its dictates. She held herself with unnatural erectness and suppressed every feminine characteristic; even allowing her black hair to hang straight, in conformance with a little-heeded state injunction against the permanent wave of the "old society." The interpreter once told me she had been educated in a Protestant middle school and had believed in Christianity until the "new science" of communism changed her.

This strange pair, and the ever-present country-boy guard, formed the audience when the religious debate finally started. The judge invited me to sit down, at the start of one session, then said, without preamble, "You know, we are not against religion."

This gave me the opening for which I had been preparing. "That isn't so," I answered. "It is refuted by your own Communist Party pamphlet on Stalin and religion. It says: 'A good communist must positively fight against religions and all other superstition.' "

The judge assumed an air of patience. "You don't quite

understand what this means," he said. "Freedom of religion means that people are free to believe it, but the Communist Party also is free to attack it."

"I know. That is like saying you are free to sleep but I am free to keep you awake by raising a racket outside your bedroom window."

Agnes looked startled, and the judge chewed hard on his candy. The interchange continued this way for a short time, then, inevitably, it swung directly into Marxism-Leninism.

"We communists," the judge said, "are not dogmatic or static—I mean, rigid—in our doctrine. We believe that everything is constantly changing, with the facts of realistic development.

"For instance," he continued, "we hope someday to do away with the Communist Party and to develop a completely classless society. So we are against the Communist Party as much as we are against superstition."

He looked pleased with himself, but, with my old debating instincts, I was just beginning to warm up to the subject.

"That is a very shrewd observation," I remarked, while the judge smirked, "except that it was not believed by Marx or Lenin or Stalin, nor is it believed by Mao." His eyes narrowed when I went on. "They taught—and all of them taught —that the basic principles of dialectics never change. These are absolute dogma." I was using the word "dialectics" in the communist sense, as meaning class struggle and class warfare.

"You recall," I continued, "that Marx said the natural laws of society are absolute, objective and predetermined by nature. They are not made by God or man, he said, and they cannot be changed by God or man. Therefore, the strategy and goal of Marxism are immutable and cannot be changed; only tactics can change, according to circumstances. Now, isn't that Marxism?"

158

"Well," the judge admitted slowly, "you have a point . . ."

"And furthermore," I added, "isn't it true theoretically that all revolution must be led by the workers and the workers must be led by the Communist Party? Therefore the goal that we're talking about is domination of the forces of revolution by the Communist Party—and that means the Communist Party can never wither away."

The judge sat back and glared at me. In the corner, the guard stood up stiffly, his mouth half open, and started fumbling with the heavy Luger in its wooden holster. Agnes, for just an instant, seemed to squint in thought, then she quickly smothered the expression.

"Perhaps I was rather careless in the way I put it," the judge admitted, after a long pause, and the tension immediately died. "Authentic communist doctrine does admit that there are changeless, absolute laws. I did not express this correctly." In fact, the changelessness of these basic concepts is the foundation of dogma, for it ensures the perpetual authority of the Communist Party.

"What the esteemed judge said," Agnes put in, with high-pitched fervor, "is perfectly understandable in the correct sense and it was for you to give it a sympathetic interpretation." The judge shot her a look of approval for this face-saving gesture.

"Since you brought up the subject," I continued, before they could recover, "there is one point of dogma which I do not understand and which I believe you can explain for me. How would the 'law of opposites' come to an end in a classless society?"

This referred to the theory, in communist mythology, that the struggle of dialectics results automatically and perpetually from the interplay of opposing forces. Each new "thesis" produces an "antithesis," the conflict between them creates a new "thesis" and the process continues. This chain reaction, the communists believe, is a law of nature, which necessarily must always be true. They can never explain how this immutable condition would disappear in the so-called classless society which they predict as the inevitable result of the world's historical forces.

"What was the question again?" the judge asked.

"How would the 'law of opposites' come to an end in a classless society?"

The judge jumped to his feet, and shouted, "Stand at attention, you fool! You are here to answer questions, not to ask them. And don't you forget that!"

Agnes and the guard chimed in with similar comments, and momentarily the drab room echoed with a medley of Chinese anger. Then the judge began a new, screaming lecture, along the old, familiar lines, and I retreated into stiff silence. Relations were back to normal.

This ended all pretense of debating religion and concluded our discussion of Marxism. Among other points, the episode illustrated how far I or any other prisoner could expect to get in a logical conversation about communism. Nevertheless, it was significant that, even though the judge lost considerable face on his own dogmatic grounds, I was not punished for my remarks, beyond the usual procedure of standing at attention.

The incident was splendid for my morale, however, and I was buoyant for days. I knew the expectable outcome before starting the Marxist argument, of course, and had no intention of trying to convert the audience. My only purpose was to take the offensive in a relatively secure battle area, in an attempt to disconcert the opposition while strengthening my own position. There always was the risk of angering the judges by such an attack, but in this case I was reasonably sure of escaping the use of greater force. There was nothing in the Marxist debate to justify changing established plans for my treatment. Higher authorities obviously had decided to avoid using direct torture on me, so the men in charge of my case could not admit their own loss of face, particularly over Marxism, by doing so. This underlines my contention that the careful prisoner can fight back effectively without greatly increasing his punishment.

It is necessary to point out, however, that the communists will not hesitate to use any form of pressure below the threshold of torture and brutality to compensate for this kind of loss of face, as well as for other purposes. This was particularly well illustrated in one of the incidents reported from a Korean prison camp. A lone American prisoner refused to accept the communist instructor's contention that South Korean forces had started the Korean War, and said so. When he continued to maintain this position, the entire class was made to stand at attention for hours, and then was told that no one would eat unless the holdout retracted his charge that North Korea had begun the conflict. He capitulated, finally, under the group pressure of his hungry buddies.*

In this case the GI's defiance to the communist "big lie" was laudable but ill-timed. He was too vulnerable to the group pressures around him to make his charge stick. Unless he could escape those pressures or, better, convince others to join him in defiance, his only adequate defense was to maintain silence. As it was, the communists no doubt believed they won that engagement because they forced him to capitulate, and the probable result was increased communist pressure in the next instance.

The type of one-man offensive I have described is beneficial to the prisoner and damaging to the communists, but it was effective only because I was relatively immune from counteraction. This immunity is impossible unless the prisoner is completely free from group pressure. I had decided

---

* Kinkead, *In Every War But One.*

consciously to free myself from any group influence, regardless of the nationality of my cellmates. Otherwise I would not have attempted overt attack.

In some ways there were more pitfalls when I turned to the use of trifles for counterattack. Since trifles usually are the only tools available, the prisoner's ability to take the offensive depends upon his capacity to recognize and avoid traps along the way. The communists will continually attempt to turn his activities against him, using any mistake as an opportunity to indict him for a prison crime or to make him admit the first damaging confession of a crime against the state.

On this level the authorities and I waged a strange little fringe war after the furor of the Marxist episode had died down. At this time a number of Red Cross parcels had arrived for me, but I had refused to accept them, despite frequent attempts by the judges to persuade me to do so. My purpose was to prevent any use of these parcels to persuade me, even subconsciously, to weaken my resistance to the authorities by crediting them for giving me my own food.

One day, however, two small parcels from a Red Cross package were shoved through the bars of my cell for me, and I had no choice but to take them out of the way of the other prisoners. One was a one-pound package of cookies and the second was a small package of assorted Swiss cheeses. Obviously, they had been delivered on orders from the authorities, but I was not sure, at first, why they had done this.

A few days later I was called from the cell late at night and told to bring my belongings with me. I bundled everything together, with the cheese and cookies on top, and in response to orders left the bundle in the cellblock corridor in the guard's charge. I was taken downtown to a special interrogation which lasted several hours. When I returned, the other five prisoners had been removed from the cell, and my pile of clothing was sitting alone in the center of the floor. The guard roughly told me to go to sleep.

In preparing to lie down, I untied my little package of clothing. Then I noticed that the cheese was missing, although everything else, including the cookies, was intact. Despite the hour, I summoned the guard immediately and told him that the cheese had been stolen. Angrily he insisted that was impossible.

"Stay there and watch," I shouted. While he stood with his nose to the peephole, I went back to my handful of possessions. Piece by piece, I took out the frayed socks and the ragged underwear, laying them down carefully on the concrete floor. I showed him the cookies, then waved my hand over the rest of the mess.

"No cheese," I said. "It's been stolen. You can see that there is no place to hide it in this empty cell."

"Shut up!" the guard said, and disappeared.

But I continued to hound him every day about the missing cheese. Although I had refused to eat it, when it was first given to me days before, this little packet now had become a weapon in my personal cold war. There was no doubt in my mind that it had been removed on orders from above. No guard or wandering trusty would have dared to take it from the bundle while it was in the custody of a representative of the People's Democratic Republic. No one else had the chance.

"The People's Democratic Republic is responsible for my cheese," I yelled at every opportunity, with my old-time obnoxiousness. "I left it in the custody of a representative of the state. Where is it?"

I made the charge every time the guard came into view and whenever I faced an interrogator. But I never went beyond the careful limits of this one accusation. By then I was convinced that the authorities had taken the cheese for more than the obvious purpose of annoying me. It was probable they wanted to goad me into directly accusing the guard of stealing the packet or of charging the interrogator with ordering the theft. Then they would wheel out another prisoner who would "confess" to taking the cheese. I would be guilty of calumniating the state, a serious charge in itself, and I would have been vulnerable to the whole process of admitting a crime and, perhaps, beginning the cycle of self-doubt and guilt.

By avoiding this specific trap, I had obtained another means of keeping the authorities off balance and on the defensive. I had planned how to use this. Even if they had returned the cheese after my first complaints, expecting gratitude, I intended to continue my protests, by accusing them of negligently permitting the disappearance of the package in the first place. As it turned out, I never saw the cheese again, so I had an issue which I could—and did—raise constantly for several months. After the first few days the authorities found themselves in a dilemma. If they returned the missing item, they would lose face by this tacit admission that they had had it all the time. The longer they delayed the more they subjected themselves to the charge of incompetence, for failing to prevent a theft in such a closely guarded jail. By not returning it at all they made themselves vulnerable to my needling and nullified any chance of profiting from the incident.

"Have you found my cheese yet?" I would ask at the start of each interrogation, and the question itself became the same type of accusation so often made, with similar indirectness, by the communists themselves.

In fact, in each of these little episodes I used the same tactics and some of the same dialogue employed by the communists in their attempts to trap the prisoner. The authorities were as incapable of resisting my attack on these petty, but important, points as were prisoners who believed themselves to be guilty of such minor infractions. The judges proved this by the way in which they tolerated my obstreperousness, by their attempts to shuttle me to another prison and by their efforts to catch me in the same kind of subtle trap. The difference, of course, was that I had no power behind me, nor any of the other weapons available to the communists. I could make a judge tacitly admit guilt over the mishandling of a box of cookies, by forcing him to display confusion and uncertainty before a mere prisoner. But I could not make this into a "crime," punishable by all the authority of a powerful state. If the positions had been reversed, however, I might have been able to brainwash the judge.

The basic point, then, is that in most cases effective brainwashing depends upon the creation of a sense of guilt, however minute it is in the beginning. This can be induced in countless ways. The so-called "fair-minded" prisoner, for instance, who says to himself that "according to their laws" he might be a spy for talking against communism is exposing himself to this erosion. The boy who was not sure why he was in Korea or was unclear about the origins of the Korean War became vulnerable to the clever communist line about "reunifying" that unhappy nation. This trap is even more cleverly baited under current conditions in Southeast Asia, where the communists have gone to great effort to create the fiction of a "popular uprising" on behalf of communism. The prisoner who hates himself for his first step toward collaboration, against the warnings of his conscious mind, or the man who informs on a cellmate is even further gone.

The only effective antidote is the self-conviction that the one constant in a communist prison is unremitting war, a war without any truce. In war it is difficult, if not impossible, to commit a crime against an enemy soldier while in combat;

and in this prison war every guard, every judge, every informer is an enemy soldier on a battlefield. Therefore, the prisoner is innocent and need feel no guilt for any of his actions. Similarly, the prisoner must adopt the same attitude toward enemy propaganda in a prison as he would in a battle where he is absolutely convinced of the justness of his cause.

This is the attitude of the communist authorities. Consequently, they do not hesitate to use any tactic, however reprehensible it might appear under what the West regards as peacetime conditions. This conviction in their own implacable war is one reason why the communists so adamantly reject every anticommunist argument given to them, while depending upon their own sweet talk to soften their less resolute prisoners. It is, moreover, the only attitude they could adopt to make brainwashing effective. Without transforming petty incidents into "crimes" and without making arrest an actual conviction, they would have few "guilty" prisoners; for none of the captives I encountered was really guilty of anything approaching a legitimate offense against the state.

The second major point of these prison vignettes is that the exaggerated fear of torture and brutality by captured prisoners often becomes their weakest point. As my experiences indicate, the amount of force used against the captives is determined by policy and not by the actions of the man himself. That is, unless he goes out of his way to invite unplanned angry reprisal. The communists encourage this fear, of course, for it is invaluable to them. The prisoner who realizes that it is an unfounded fear, however, can save himself much mental torture and can strengthen his own resolve immeasurably.

In my case, a knowledge of the communist and the Chinese character undoubtedly proved valuable, because it permitted

166

me to conduct a vigorous offensive without overstepping the invisible boundary which divides strength from insufferable overbearing, in the Asian concept. I avoided trouble in the fracas over the cheese because I refrained from accusing anyone directly of theft. In the case of the cookies, I could condemn the first judge because, on the basis of logic, he had made a mistake. But he was not present to defend himself, and the second judge would have lost an unacceptable amount of face by bringing this mistake to the attention of higher authorities. Face has exaggerated influence on communists and Asians generally, including the Soviets. But some elements of this concept are present in every society. In the end, the use of face is more a matter of common sense than particular training, and I am confident anyone can learn it quickly.

Through these and other methods I was able to counter and reduce the pressures on me for a confession. But the communists never abandoned their effort to extract one from me, for their major reason in imprisoning me was to obtain a signed admission of my crimes. This effort cost them many hundreds of man-hours, a factor underlining the importance of confessions to them.

Chapter eight

THE PHONY
FAÇADE

THE ELABORATE PROCEDURES USED BY THE
Chinese communists to obtain a "voluntary" confession
are part of a comprehensive attempt to legalize and to justify
nearly everything they do. Peking is very conscious of the
façade it has erected to mask its operations, and the authorities go out of their way to perpetuate and strengthen it. A
voluntary confession is another stone in this wall of respectability.

Duplicity, under the communist state, begins actually with
the most fundamental concept, the myth that the hundreds
of thousands of bureaucrats who run the country have come
from the ranks of the "workers." The significance of this idea
was illustrated for me, with comic effect, during one of my
recurrent assignments to the Loukawei prison. Despite the

alleged preponderance of workers in this teeming nation, the ceiling above our grimy, smelly cell had been scarred for weeks by a large hole in the plaster. It remained there without attention until one of the guards, who slept in the cell above us, complained. Then the matter was handled with bustling urgency one humid day.

The "plasterer," it turned out, was not an outside workman, but the assistant warden who had spit in my face during the first debate over religion early in my imprisonment. He darted into the cell, breathing arrogance and cigarette smoke, while an accompanying soldier staggered under a vast collection of trowels, brushes, water, ladder, and a bucket of plaster. The warden ceremoniously set to work, with pomp and confidence. He was inordinately proud of being a "workingman."

At the time I was clamped between the two violently anti-American prisoners who had nearly driven me crazy. They began a litany of praise for the warden as soon as he appeared, and maintained it continually during the repair job. As the official troweled the ceiling with sweeping, artistic strokes, one of the prisoners shouted in my ear, "This shows the humility and the true working spirit of our officials." The warden slapped harder at the ceiling. "Yes," said the second prisoner, "we are very fortunate to be led by men of such outstanding capability." The warden glowed appreciatively as he continued his task and made no effort to enforce the rule of silence, which was supposed to be in effect.

Finally, the warden completed the job with a great farewell flourish and stepped down from the ladder. He stood momentarily in the middle of the cell, admiring his workmanship, while the prisoners talked on. "Such sweeping strokes." "And so efficient." When the soldier had collected all the paraphernalia, the official thrust his head back proudly and, with a final baleful glance at me, strode toward the heavy iron door. As a final gesture of authority, he slammed the door with terrific force. The cell floor shook—and the complete plaster job plopped to the floor. For once, my annoying cellmates were caught wordless.

Not all of the activities of the People's Dictatorship are this inefficient or humorous, but most of them are equally hypocritical.

All the paper currency now in circulation, for instance, bears the legend, "The Chinese People's Republic," in four languages—Chinese, Mongolian, Uigur and Tibetan. The purpose is to show the significance of these four racial groups and to support Peking's elaborate contention that all the minority races in this polyglot nation enjoy equality. This gesture was handled with such attention to detail that Uigur was elevated to major status, although it is spoken by only about three million people in a population of more than six hundred million. The Uigurs are people of Turkish stock who inhabit the northwest province of Sinkiang, an area which, incidentally, long has been in dispute between the Russians and the Chinese. The Tibetans, particularly, must have found scant consolation in this recognition when the new currency was issued in 1955, a few years after Peking began its bloody campaign to conquer and dominate that remote mountain country. The Chinese communists crushed the 1959 revolt in Tibet so brutally that an international commission of jurists formally reported that planned genocide was used to subdue the Tibetans.

Red China also remains the only communist nation with a number of officially recognized noncommunist political parties. They go by such names as the Revolutionary Committee of the Kuomintang, the China Democratic League, the China Association for Promoting Democracy, and the Taiwan Democratic Self-Government League. All are represented in the People's Congress and several of their leaders have occupied ministerial posts in the large Chinese communist cabinet. Periodically, these parties join in well-propagandized support for some popular communist issue, such as a strong endorsement in August, 1962, of the thesis that American nuclear tests were abominable but those detonated by Soviet Russia were necessary to preserve peace. In practice, these parties have no independence, and it was notable that most of them and their leaders were sharply attacked for deviation during the purge campaign that followed the "Hundred Flowers" period of freedom of speech in 1957.

The same charade is played with labor unions, cultural groups, and to some extent, religious organizations; all used to advertise the "benevolence" and "freedom" of the Chinese communist government. An admonition to labor organizations, published by the Peking *Daily Worker* on November 9, 1960, carried a flat and clear order to all these noncommunist groups. "The interests of the state, the collective interests," the editorial said, "must be regarded as your own interests, their business as your own business. The construction of the country must be done by our own strength, with effort, bitter struggle and thrift . . . by hard work, by listening to the orders of the Party, going where the Party directs, doing what the Party wants." The reference, of course, was to the Communist Party.

In one of my prisons we received the rare privilege of being served one or two ounces of pork once every six or eight weeks. Before this meal, the guard carefully would canvass the prisoners to determine the number of Mohammedans among them, and they would be given fish instead. This ritual was conducted seriously and with considerable ceremony, as a gesture of religious tolerance and thoughtfulness; although numerous Catholic priests had been killed, missionaries of all Christian faiths repeatedly had been tortured, churches and schools were confiscated, and the gospels could not be taught in public.

Much more than the propaganda impact of so-called religious and political tolerance was involved, however. The Chinese people were subject to the manipulation of these disguised organizations, and therefore their perpetuation had a useful purpose. Conversely, the Chinese concern over face made it unlikely that the leaders of these groups would defy both their followers and the authorities to advocate policies unwelcome to the state. If they did, the mere application of group condemnation usually was sufficient to bring the leadership back into line. Under these conditions, Peking could exercise more control over noncommunist politicians by permitting them to operate openly than by driving them underground.

But it is also probable, I believe, that this façade became necessary to satisfy the strong sense of face and the fierce desire for international recognition by the Communist Party leaders. They gained prestige, at home and abroad, by this apparent benevolence, although it did not appear necessary as a means of placating any strong demands from the people. The Peking authorities have made little effort to hide their chagrin over the fact that Russia is accepted as a major power while Red China is still seeking admission to international society. On the other hand, they do not attempt to hide their pleasure whenever a visiting foreign dignitary or correspondent reports favorably to his own country on the "social progress" of the Peking regime. The importance of praise to Peking and its hatred of criticism are emphasized by the fact that it carefully screens the writers it admits and excludes most Americans, even though it would receive invaluable publicity by permitting a dozen or so American correspondents to travel throughout the country.

This preoccupation with the proper façade is a general Asian characteristic. The Chinese communists, like many other Asians, seem to believe that if the screen is proper even the most unworthy action behind it will go unnoticed. Moreover, Peking no doubt would reject any suggestion that the prestige it covets would come more quickly through benevolent actions than bogus legalities. Instead, it is possible that the communist leaders regard sincere benevolence as a sign of weakness, and therefore a loss of face, if not a violation of Marxism-Leninism.

Some of these ideas were swirling through my head on a warm Sunday afternoon when an unusual bustle in the prison announced that preparations were being made to receive a special visitor. At the time, I was being kept in the hospital of Ward Road jail, on my second sojourn in that brooding fortress. For some unexplained reason, the authorities decided to give me fairly decent quarters and, for the first time, three meals a day, while practicing another form of coercion on me.

My cell had a window overlooking the courtyard, and I could see a large crew of trusties hurriedly cleaning the yard. With a great clatter, they quickly gathered the more than 5,000 filthy tin cans used to feed us and which were stacked on little flatcars to transport them on miniature railroad tracks from the prison kitchen. I knew the precise number because I had whiled away some of my time counting them. Other trusties worked with equal frenzy to hose down and mop the cellblock corridors and to complete other preparations. Guards rounded up a group of about a hundred prisoners who, crippled from beri-beri, were allowed in the courtyard for a few minutes of sunshine each day, and herded them into the convalescent cellblock.

Soon, the prison almost sparkled, and I thought it must have looked halfway presentable—from the outside. In time, a crowd of officials appeared in the courtyard, surrounding a foreign visitor of indeterminable nationality. No doubt, they were explaining the "merits" of their prison system to him. The visitor spent a short period viewing the newly scrubbed jail and listening to his hosts. Then he disappeared. I never learned his identity, nor could I ascertain what he reported to the outside world about Ward Road jail.

But if he did not comment on the prison upon his return home he probably would have been the first foreigner of any nationality to display such reticence. If he came from a Western nation, the chances are that he spoke rather well of the jail, as so many other visitors have done, because he could see nothing but its well-turned façade.

At that moment, however, I was undergoing the most harrowing experience of my imprisonment.

For several weeks the authorities had increased their pressures to force me into a confession or, at least, into a form of cooperation useful for propaganda. Dehumanization had been intensified, and so had the threats of dire punishment. But the authorities also attempted to coax me into taking some of the food contained in a large number of Red Cross parcels that had arrived for me. Letters from my aged mother had been delivered, after much delay, with the repeated comment, "We know that your mother has written often to you; wouldn't you like to go home and see her?" Finally, they had begun a serious effort to get me to visit their factory districts, to observe "how we have built up China." I refused these obvious propaganda overtures.

When I maintained my stubborn opposition, the judges could not hide their frustration and anger. "You cannot re-educate a blockhead!" one muttered despairingly, after another half-hour lecture. Finally, I was sent to the hospital at Ward Road jail, the most pleasant—or least objectionable— quarters I had occupied in more than two years. When food began arriving three times daily, I found myself caught between a glimmer of hope that release was near and the stronger suspicion that I was being subjected to a particularly tantalizing form of the "sweet treatment."

I shared a sort of "suite" of two small adjoining cells with two other prisoners, who had become so progressive that they were given daily papers and large quantities of other "literature," mostly propaganda. Both of them took great delight in reading aloud and recounting with particular stridency all the charges made against the United States and the Catholic Church in the condemnatory articles that regularly constituted "news." With only a moderate amount of practice, they succeeded in becoming nearly as obnoxious as my two previous anti-American cellmates. This time, however, I was prepared. Whenever my companions began reading aloud, I started singing—and my voice is terrible. It was questionable who annoyed whom the most.

But this was not the primary reason for my assignment to the prison hospital. On the first night, when I was about to congratulate myself on the improved circumstances, a hauntingly familiar moan began in an adjacent cell. It came from poor old Wu, the maniac with whom I had been confined in the padded cell nearly two years before. For all that time, this unfortunate man had been screeching out his inner torment every night; frightening other communist victims, no doubt, but finding no release from his own devils. "Oh, if I had only confessed!" he screamed. "Oh, if I had only confessed!" Boom-boom, boom-boom! All night, he went on, with the same chilling tones, the same horrible mental flagellation.

Wu began with a distant, strangled moan, as if he were confined some distance away, but on successive nights his symphony of terror grew closer and closer, until it seemed he was about to burst into our cell. He was closest and loudest whenever the judges made their most intensive efforts to get me on a propaganda factory trip. So it was clear the authorities were using this unfortunate man not only to wear away my resolve but also to express their own condemnation of my obdurate refusal to become a propaganda tool.

There was more. After two months of this, a second maniac began working the day shift. When Wu finally subsided into exhausted impotence, the new man awoke refreshed to his own private world of horror. "Do not do that!" he cried. "Please do not do that! I will do anything you want—only do not do that!" Then he would scream and moan and cry with great, gasping sobs. All day he fought off the terror that was too much for him to mention; all day he poured out his agony. Listening to the endless cries of these two men, I had to summon my last bit of resolve to control the inevitable sense of hopelessness created by this terror.

This cacophony lasted for a month, almost incessantly, and I had virtually no sleep during that period. Whenever the moans subsided, there was always the guard's pounding club or the loud and annoying ridicule of my cellmates. It was clear the authorities had transferred me to the hospital so I would be next to the maniacs' padded cells. At the same time, however, the food was more plentiful and other circumstances also were better.

Among other "improvements," my cell had a large window and, for once, the customary wooden boards had been removed, permitting some air. For the first time I slept on a bed. I was taken out of the cell into the fresh air and sunshine for a fifteen-minute exercise period each day. These were welcome changes, despite the maniacs, and I savored them. But they were done for a clearly identifiable purpose. The boards were taken from the cell window, for instance, so that I could hear the maniacs' shrieks more loudly. The only space allowed me for exercise was alongside the padded cells, and I had to listen to the ravings while enjoying this privilege.

Still, this did not completely explain the new treatment.

176

The judge's rage was understandable when I refused to fall into his trap to visit the factories and thus lend myself to propaganda. But why should he rage when I refused my own Red Cross parcels? Why was all this so important that the maniacs were brought closer and stimulated to yell louder in reprisal? Why was I given extra food and a bed while intimidation was increased?

There may be many explanations, but when I put the circumstances together, while the yowling went on around me, I could find only one logical reason: the mixture of "sweet and sour" was being deliberately made richer. At the very least, I thought, the pressure was intensified to warn me that I might be returned to my padded cell alongside Wu. Perhaps the purpose was to show me again that I was not immune from ending up like Wu. At worst, this could have been a planned application of direct Pavlovism.

If so, it seemed highly significant that progressives had been assigned as my cellmates; for, of course, they also endured Wu's howls. Watching my companions closely, I saw little evidence that the maniacal shrieks bothered them nearly as much as they did me. Instead, they seemed to take refuge in the comforting embrace of propaganda and communist bromides and to draw strength from their reliance on the state. The hatred they showed toward me, by reading derogatory editorials and by direct insult, seemed to stimulate them and to make the environment more bearable for them. Perhaps, this, too, was intended as a warning of what I might become. Certainly, the state's ability to retain their allegiance while subjecting them to this treatment was a demonstration of communist power over the minds and emotions of these men.

As for me, I confess that this period became more difficult to endure because of the Pavlovian extremes. Being comparatively well fed made the insults of my companions more annoying. The daily glimpse of sunshine exaggerated the horror of Wu's nightly chorus. Quite literally, I did not know what to expect when summoned by the judge, for he had shown me a wider range of reward and punishment than I had encountered up to that time. It took even greater effort than before to withstand this combination of soft and hard treatment and to maintain my obduracy. But the communists failed to make one important calculation: with practice, my stubbornness also had become immeasurably stronger.

These were my circumstances when the unidentified foreigner visited our hastily scrubbed jail that Sunday afternoon. I remembered the day with particular clarity for another reason. Wu and his traveling companion could not be heard, for the first time in weeks, while the foreigner was present, and the sudden silence was, indeed, blessed. Their moans could be cut off by closing heavy iron doors designed for that purpose. The maniacs also could be silenced by a sharp order from the guard, so great was their fear. The screeching resumed, of course, when the official visit was finished.

The visitor knew nothing of this, naturally, and the authorities made sure he did not find out about it. In ways such as these the Chinese communists have induced a number of Western visitors to describe approvingly the "advances" in penology and the improvement in prisoner treatment under the Peking regime. This is understandable, because the façade is so carefully tended and because visiting Westerners always are under the guidance of the authorities, whether they realize it or not. This particular foreigner probably saw as much of the Ward Road jail during his brief visit as the average noncommunist traveler in Red China sees of the country itself. Manifestly, this is insufficient evidence upon which to base an opinion.

The whole question of law and penal practices is so fundamental in the assessment of the Peking government that misleading observations can be serious. One commentator who visited Ward Road jail at a different period, for instance, reported that it held only 2,400 prisoners and that it was the only jail in Shanghai, a city of six million persons. The implication was that the communist regime had succeeded in reducing actual crime to a minor problem and that the regime had won such general support that it no longer needed to confine large numbers of political prisoners. Acceptance of these suggestions, in turn, means greater trust than warranted in both the popularity and the benevolence of the communist regime. In other words, the façade becomes the reality. Actually, Ward Road jail has more than 4,000 cells and in 1956 housed more than 15,000 prisoners. Two of the other prisons in which I was confined had a normal capacity of 2,000 prisoners each. Loukawei was actually only a small guardhouse, with space for 60 to 70 men. In addition, each police station in Shanghai can handle 100 prisoners at a time. Under the communists, the prison population fluctuated widely. By overcrowding, however, they were able to increase these figures by several times in order to accommodate the victims of periodic roundups, as my own experiences have shown.

A widespread misconception of Peking's approach to its own people and its methods of treating them also can be of great international significance. It involves the fundamentals of whether the West should deal diplomatically with the Chinese communist regime and, if so, on what terms. If Peking is benevolent at home, there is a chance it may act that way internationally. But it is difficult to see how domestic brutality in the name of a political belief can be muted into sincere international collaboration. Correct appraisal of the façade, therefore, becomes of prime importance.

This point had been impressed on me with particular clarity a few months earlier. In the blistering heat of September, 1955, I was transferred suddenly back to my worst prison, Massenet, in the heart of the French Concession. This crumbling old jail was sunk in the bustle of a crowded street only a stone's throw from my own church. Inside the scarred prison walls, however, captives crossed the River Styx into another world.

At Massenet, I was put in a fourth-floor cell with five other men, although the total space was only about 5 by 8 feet. We were so crowded that it was impossible to lie at full length, and when we tried to sleep, the whole room had to turn over to accommodate one restless man. Ironically, the authorities allotted ten hours each night for "rest," from 7 P.M. to 5 A.M. Despite the intense heat—and Shanghai can be hotter than New York City in September—there was no ventilation in the cell, and we steamed in our own body glow. At feeding times, twice daily, we were given congee, rice in hot water, with a few old string beans. While we ate, the temperature within the cell seemed to increase by 5 to 10 degrees.

Each morning a shallow pan of water was placed on the cellblock floor, outside the bars, and each man dipped his filthy towel into it for face-washing. As usual, I was last. In the three months since my last bath, my body had been covered from shaved head to calloused feet with prickly heat, small boils and infected splotches. The sanitary arrangements were indescribably crude, and our cell was quite literally a pigpen.

Worst of all, the cells were infested with what the Chinese call a "stink bug," a bloodsucking insect which seemed to be a cross between a bedbug and a tick. These bugs would swarm from the wooden floors each night, to feast on the inmates, scurrying back to their hideouts in the predawn light. The bugs who failed to make it were plastered across the walls, and this condition had persisted so long that the walls were covered, from floor to ceiling, with smeared human blood.

In this "bucket of blood," the tempo of petty annoyances from the guards noticeably increased, with obvious deliberateness. This attitude was reflected in every way, from the accumulated filth of the surroundings to intensified harassment of each captive. Yet each of my fellow prisoners had "solved his case"—presumably through confession—and had received his sentence.

Prison terms ran from ten to twenty years, and those with the longest sentences spent much of the day bemoaning their fate. I never knew whether they also realized that the authorities were demonstrating their contempt for confessed enemies by increasing the intensity of mental torture.

Three days after my arrival I was summoned for interrogation. The date was September 12, 1955—as computed by my now reliable mental calendar—and, I learned later, it had particular significance. Entering the familiar bare and neglected interrogation room, I confronted a judge new to my case but a man who evidently outranked all my other interrogators. He had appeared as a sort of observer on a few previous occasions, and his influence was indicated by the obsequiousness shown him by the regular judges.

Mentally I had nicknamed him Fang, for his thin lips were curled perpetually into a sneer which exposed a long, yellow tooth. He was tall for a Chinese, gaunt and slightly stooped. Entering sallow middle age, he constantly burped slightly, as if from an ulcer, and chain-smoking had yellowed his fingers. But his cold, hard eyes reflected a sense of power and cruelty. He had made it plain with a few sharp comments on previous occasions that he was completely confident he had the skill to "break my case."

Seated at his bare desk, Fang met me with the hard, penetrating stare often used by Asians to disconcert their inferiors. While I stood silent, at attention, I noticed there were two guards in the room, both with drawn pistols. The judge was flanked by a girl interpreter, another acquaintance of mine from the long interrogations of the past, whom I had named Dolly. She was, if you will, the "glamour girl" of the communist army; a cute and comparatively chic youngster in her early twenties. Even in bulbous army uniform she retained some of her femininity, but on this occasion she was downright counterrevolutionary. Dolly wore a gaily printed dress, clean and neatly pressed, and the corners of her bobbed hair were slightly curled, in defiance of the state's injunctions against such "frivolity."

"I must warn you," Fang began, staring at me with icy eyes, "that this is absolutely your last chance to settle your case. You can still win clemency by confessing. Otherwise . . ." his voice dropped, and he sat there glowering.

"I am an innocent Catholic priest, persecuted because of my religion," I said firmly, as I had several hundred times previously.

"No," Fang shouted, "you are an enemy of the state, and I will prove it to you." Then for the next ten minutes or so he read a résumé of my career in China, pausing frequently and motioning for Dolly to translate. She did this with considerable skill and evident pride in her ability. The details of this familiar story were the same as I had recounted more than two years before and, of course, no more condemnatory in my eyes now than originally.

"Now," said Fang, hunching over the desk, "you must realize the enormity of your crimes. This is positively your last chance to confess." He stared in silence, puffing on a cigarette while Dolly translated, but he paid such close attention to the English version that it seemed evident he understood the language.

"The people's government has been very patient with you," Fang resumed, "but its patience is not inexhaustible. If you do not confess now, if you do not settle your case when you have this opportunity—you will feel the just wrath of the people's government." He let that seep through, then added, "Quite frankly, you will be given the harshest possible sentence."

"I am an innocent Catholic priest, persecuted—"

"No!" Fang shouted, jumping to his feet. "You cannot insult the People's Court this way!" He spun quickly around the desk and snorted, "You are a fool!" Dolly also rose, and added some comments of her own while translating the judge's insulting remark. She was no longer chic nor dainty, but a hard little hellcat.

Both of them screamed sloganized epithets at me in harsh, raucous voices, and I recoiled from this sudden and unexpected attack. The guards rushed to flank me, their huge guns waving in front of them. Both of them kicked at my ankles and calves with their heavy army shoes, shouting, "Stand erect!" "Show more respect, you worm!"

For several minutes, all four of them surrounded me, shouting and cursing with the crackling venom that Mandarin can convey. Fang became particularly abusive, standing in front of me and looking down from his greater height, with his thin, leering face a few inches from my own. "You will suffer for this," he snarled, "you will suffer—se ti—enemy until death!" As his anger increased, so did his stomach distress, and he coughed out his insults; and consequently they became more menacing.

I fought to maintain my composure, for I was genuinely worried. The insults and threats were difficult enough to endure under any conditions, but this quartet managed to infuse a sense of sincerity into them which had been missing from my past experiences with the carefully staged anger of my interrogators. Fang's choleric attack convinced me that he felt a personal loss of face because he had been so confident of breaking me. Therefore, it was easy to believe that the communists meant what they said.

Gradually, the others pulled back and subsided into muttering, but Fang continued without letup to flay me with his anger. He circled around me like a beast, stalking with his peculiar slouch and stopping only to glare into my face and spit out his insults directly at me.

"I have the power," he yelled, "to sentence you right here and now to twenty years in prison, and if you do not cooperate, I will do it. What good will your capitalist friends be then? What will they do for you?"

Still shouting, he circled once more, and his insults became more venomous against me and against the United States. "You American imperialists boast so much," he snorted, "you have so much power. Where is it? Bah, you are nothing but a paper tiger!"

His anger mounted and his shouts grew louder, while the others also resumed their insults. I began to feel my knees shaking again, and it took all my strength to remain still and silent. Fang reached a new crescendo, then suddenly he stopped. The silence rushed over the bare room, with its sneering occupants, and struck me almost like a fresh insult.

"If you do not confess," Fang began once more, in low, calculated tones, "I will sentence you to death!"

He stopped, looking sharply at me, and the silence hung once more like heavy fog.

My knees slumped slightly, and I said a fervent mental prayer. I believed Fang implicitly, for there was no doubting the genuineness of his anger or the scope of his authoritarian power. Nothing could save me, I realized, from this ugly, arrogant man's wrath.

This was the first time the death sentence had been mentioned explicitly, although others had hinted at it. By such directness, I thought, Fang had warned me that the least I could expect would be interminable imprisonment, with execution most probable.

Yet, with the quickness of thought which danger produces, I also realized that this was the authorities' last card. They could go no further by way of threats. I had defied them successfully thus far, and I had been desperately afraid before. All the torment of the last twenty-six months would be wasted and lost if I capitulated now.

Wordlessly, I shook my head.

Fang erupted into immediate anger. Again circling me, he poured out fresh bile, and repeated his threats. Dolly screamed at me once more with hard, relentless fanaticism. The guards moved alongside me, waving those giant revolvers with annoying carelessness.

In all, the tirade lasted perhaps forty minutes. Finally, Fang sat down at his desk and stared at me for a long moment with evident disbelief. Then he waved me away.

The guards hurried me back to the bucket of blood and shoved me roughly through the barred door. When I had slumped down in my narrow place on the floor I began to tremble and could not stop. My cellmates paid no attention while I sat there, sweating, shaking and praying. Even this stinking, red-splotched pen was a refuge.

Two days later I was again called for interrogation, and once more I noted the date—September 14, 1955. I plodded toward the bare room with strongly clashing emotions. My resolve had been strengthened during the past forty-eight hours, when I had been left alone, but I could not avoid the stab of apprehension when the new summons came. I expected the worst, and tried to prepare myself for it.

Fang greeted me with undisguised triumph on his face. Beside him, Dolly looked up smugly at me, and I noted that she wore her floppy uniform, as if the occasion were special. Even the flat-faced peasant guards seemed to reflect a new sense of their power.

"I have on official announcement to read to you," Fang said, and my spirits sank. Everything had been arranged, it seemed, for the final denouement of my case, and I could only calculate that this meant at least a long sentence.

Instead, Fang read a rather detailed statement about an agreement reached in Geneva between the United States and the People's Republic of China for a mutual exchange of prisoners. I was so unprepared for this that I could neither believe nor understand the announcement, so I asked him to read it again. Only then was it clear to me that the United States and Communist China had been conducting diplomatic negotiations, on terms of equality, for some time, although I had been told nothing about them. The result was a supposedly binding arrangement for the immediate transfer of Chinese and American prisoners.

"When was the agreement signed?" I asked.

"Now you see how benevolent the people's government really is, to accept such an agreement," Fang said proudly, ignoring my question.

"When was it signed?"

"Well, now, let me see. Oh, yes. It says here that the agreement was formally endorsed on September 10."

In other words, the pact had become effective two days before Fang threatened me with death in a final attempt to break me. I had been transferred into the despair of Massenet one day before the formal signing ceremony, at a time when the details of the prisoner exchange already had been accepted by both sides. So after agreeing to repatriate the Americans, Peking set out on its final campaign to extract a confession from me, and no doubt the other American prisoners, by every possible means short of physical violence. Fang and Dolly and the guards must have known this when they staged their extremely convincing display of wrath.

Now they made no attempt to hide their pride and jubilation, because the agreement itself marked a landmark on Peking's route toward international recognition. It was, in their eyes, a small but definite sign that the United States had to deal with Communist China as a sovereign and powerful state—as an equal. In fact, these Chinese showed that they regarded the agreement as a considerable victory; probably for this reason, but also because it served to enlarge the façade of respectability. In order to regain her own emaciated and eroded citizens, the United States had to agree to "permit" the return to Red China of any Chinese desiring to do so. I also learned how vigorously Peking had been propagandizing the theme that many of its "loyal" citizens had been kept by force from leaving the United States. The purpose, quite clearly, was to build up Red China's respectability by imputing to American authorities the same savage treatment of foreign prisoners for which Peking recently had been sharply condemned. In Chinese eyes, American acceptance of the agreement confirmed the charge and absolved the Chinese from blame for their own actions.

Fang was particularly triumphant. "You would not believe me," he said, "when I told you that the United States one day would have to admit the power of the Chinese People's Republic. Well, now, you see. And it will not be long before the American imperialists will have to accept us as equal in everything." He chuckled. "But enough of that. The agreement has been made, and in time you can go home. You should be happy."

Happy? My spirits were at the lowest point of any time in my imprisonment. Although I did not know all the facts that I learned later, I realized that it was a one-sided agreement and would remain so. Having created the façade, the Chinese communists would act as they wished behind it, unless forced by superior power to carry out their commitments. Therefore, I had no assurance of release but, instead, rather convincing reasons to believe that the authorities were by no means through with me. On the other hand, the United States would scrupulously observe any applicable provisions, as usual.

For these reasons I felt at the time that, for humanitarian reasons, the United States had committed what might have been a serious diplomatic blunder; by giving a measure of recognition to Peking in exchange for tenuous promises on which total performance was doubtful. In the aftermath of Fang's announcement, I felt as if the cause for which I tried to fight so hard and so long—inflexible opposition to the communists—suddenly had been snatched from me; leaving me in a meaningless battle. To prevent any concession to the communists, I felt I would have spent the rest of my life in the bucket of blood.

The communist authorities began to implement the agreement in about the way I expected. During the next month, while I remained in Massenet, they attempted with unusual emphasis to convince me that, international pact or not, I was by no means out of danger or near freedom. Shortly after being told of the Geneva arrangement, I was hauled from jail one night and whisked across town. I found myself in the rather formal courtroom setting of the headquarters for the public prosecutor—or district attorney—of Shanghai. Here, five judges demanded a confession and, when I refused, all five began a vigorous tongue-lashing which lasted for several hours. Once more I was threatened with harsh punishment, unless I would admit my crimes and thereby settle my case. This performance was repeated again a few nights later, and the same warning continually was given to me by jail guards.

Under the Geneva agreement, any American in Red China was to be allowed to leave the country immediately if he so desired. In case of any difficulty, he was to be permitted to contact representatives of the British government wherever they might be stationed in China. The same provisions applied to Chinese in the United States, with Indian diplomatic representatives as intermediaries.

Fang had given me these details, so I demanded release mainly to give the communists an opportunity to repudiate their agreement. The guard only laughed at me. Then I demanded to see the British representative in Shanghai, the equivalent of a consul, or the British chargé d'affaires in Peking. No response. It was clear, as I had anticipated, that the Chinese had no intention of observing the terms of the agreement until, or unless, they considered compliance profitable to them. Nevertheless, I continued to insist upon my useless "rights," as a further way of annoying the authorities.

But by the time I was transferred from Massenet in October, 1955, I had lost all confidence in the willingness of the Chinese to observe the agreement in my case. If there was always a flicker of hope for release whenever the guards told me to gather up my belongings for a new move, it had by this time become a sadly shriveled hope which was quickly extinguished. I was sent first to the regular prison quarters of Ward Road jail, then in late December, 1955, transferred to the hospital ward, to be nearer Wu and his coworker. I remained there until May, 1956.

So the Chinese kept me in jail for nine months after solemnly agreeing to the release of all Americans. Throughout this period they intensified the pressures and the degradation, taking care only to make sure that no physical scars would show when I was eventually released. Although at the time I expected to remain indefinitely in jail, it now seems evident the authorities had decided at the time of the Geneva agreement on the actual date for releasing all the American priests. All that happened during these last nine months, then, was part of a planned final gesture by the communists.

In my case, I am convinced they intensified Pavlovism in

a last attempt to extract a confession or, failing that, to vent their frustration over my stubbornness. It may be they also hoped, if possible, to weaken me sufficiently so that, ever afterward, I would respond to any communist threat with unnatural fear, thereby contributing my little bit to an exaltation of their power.

Whatever the purpose, the authorities, acting under Peking's direct orders, clearly revealed their opinion of solemn international agreements. They failed to carry out all the carefully written provisions, for even today they have not released all their American prisoners. They defied the humanitarian spirit of the accord with cynical blatancy. They interpreted "immediate release" in their own way, and took advantage of protracted delays to seek every last moment of profit or vengeance.

Yet this agreement was, in fact, an extremely important precedent for Peking in its undisguised quest for international stature. It was a clear-cut and direct accord between the United States and the communist government, reached on terms of equality. If Peking expected to qualify for international acceptance on the basis of behavior, it would be logical to expect that it would observe the pact with scrupulous detail. By violating it so callously the communist leaders proved, to my mind at least, that they count only on power to gain their cherished world recognition. They confirmed their own definition: "International law is one of the instruments in international problems. When this instrument is useful to us, we use it; when this instrument is of no use to us, we use other instruments." *

I have no doubt that the American officials who arranged the prisoner exchange knew the risks of such an arrangement and accepted them as the only means of freeing the majority of the Americans illegally jailed by Peking. It is evident also

* Peking *People's Daily*, Sept. 18, 1957.

that Washington continues to deal realistically with the Chinese communists, despite pressures for recognizing them. Recognition, in my opinion, would only lead to the same kind of international arrogance which the authorities demonstrated after the Geneva accord.

The danger, however, is that the façade may become more credible as time goes on and more and more people may be willing to accept it as reality, through either hope or misinformation. On the international level, this could lead to concessions which, I believe, would only make Peking more dangerous. On the individual level, the most difficult problem for the lone American prisoner often is to recognize geniality, softness and cooperation by communist authorities as the façade they actually are. His only salvation, and the essential starting point for effective resistance, is the inflexible, constant realization that there is no such thing as a "good" communist. It may be unfortunate but it is literally true that any communist displaying characteristics of benevolence, in terms of Western morality, is either playing a role or renouncing communism itself. His dogma and his own brainwashing have been carefully contrived and perfected over the years, to set him against every moral precept of the noncommunist world. Dogma permits the communist to act like a moral human for a purpose, but it does not permit him to think that way. Once he does so he must abandon communism, for the two worlds are incompatible. Marxism-Leninism, as now preached, is designed to perpetuate this inflexible incompatability.

In Chinese communist hands, benevolence, in fact, is merely another weapon to enslave man.

Chapter nine

SWEET
AND SOUR

THE COMMUNIST AUTHORITIES PLANNED
their final campaign of "benevolence" toward me as
carefully as their program of intimidation. The two weapons
were delicately meshed and always kept in balance. It was
clear the authorities depended more upon force than leniency
to accomplish their purpose, and so the main aim of their
little kindnesses was to enlarge the impact of force. For the
last year of my imprisonment, the judges made periodic efforts
to appear benign, and throughout this period the pressures of
intimidation were constant.

Although it was not apparent at the time, the final campaign of sweetness actually began in the middle of 1955,
when I was confined with the seventeen progressives in the
discussion group cell at South City jail. Two of the judges

who continually wandered around the cellblock entered our pen one night in an unusually affable mood. Like other Chinese, the communists can be extremely polite and friendly when they wish. On this occasion the judges, whose manner during interrogation periods was as vitriolic as their compatriots, might have been solicitous uncles.

They talked pleasantly with each prisoner, asking him how he was faring and what wishes he had, as if the hot, odorous cell were a hotel room. The ragged progressives responded as might be imagined, with fulsome praise for the kindness of the visitors and modest requests for soap.

"And what do you need?" one of the judges smilingly asked me.

"Nothing. Nothing at all."

"How much soap do you have?"

I showed him a piece about the size of a half dollar.

"I can get you more," the judge said.

"No, thank you. This will do."

He looked at me quizzically, shook his head and hurried out with his companion. They returned in a few minutes. Ignoring me completely, they walked through the cell, distributing fat bars of soap to all the other prisoners.

This finale confirmed my belief that the judges were trying to establish a form of liaison with the prisoners which I had to avoid. Nevertheless, it was a difficult decision to reach, and even harder to maintain, for at that point soap was one of the immeasurable luxuries. I had been for weeks without a bath or without a chance to wash my clothes. In this condition, where self-loathing was impossible to avoid, soap became one of the important measures of life.

The communist official who could supply this unattainable necessity automatically assumed great power in the eyes of the benefiting prisoner. The official became a friend—or could become one—for his kindness, and the tendency to

193

reach out for this friendship and to rely on it could, if unchecked, be the beginning of disaster. Surrounded by enemies and by fellow victims he cannot trust, the prisoner almost subconsciously seeks friendship and then finds himself desperately trying to retain it by cooperation. Even if the prisoner continues to refuse cooperation, the anger and hatred of his new "friend" suddenly becomes more difficult to bear.

The little things that occur during imprisonment, often with apparently irrational timing, follow this formula. When a prisoner has been sufficiently dehumanized, the slightest gesture becomes meaningful. After being required to stand at attention for hours, for instance, the judge often would invite me to sit down, and I could feel a stir of gratitude. Frequently he held out a cigarette to me knowing that, if I took it, some act of cooperation would be necessary to obtain the next one.

The communists also used this lure to probe as deeply into my subconscious mind as before they had used an informer's interest in astronomy in an attempt to create guilt. In this same cell, where the progressives frequently tried to talk to me under orders from higher-ups, several of them began a curious line of questioning. They asked me first to explain the measurements of ounces and grams in terms understandable to the Chinese. Then they asked me pointed questions about several obscure cities in the United States, most particularly Kalamazoo, Michigan. Puzzled, I answered as best I could without detecting the reason for their directed interest in these subjects.

It turned out that the authorities were being somewhat too subtle. They intended as their major sweet tactic to bribe me with the Red Cross parcels that had begun arriving for me some time before. These were weighed in ounces and grams and some had been packed at Kalamazoo. The prompting of my cellmates' inquiries was supposed to develop in me an overwhelming desire for the food contained in the parcels. In my unfamiliarity with the food parcel system, I had missed the cue.

Consequently, I had developed no great hunger by the time the authorities began to implement their strategy. On another point, however, they had been more correct in their strategy. I had begun to think about my health, because I had experienced dizzy spells and unusual periods of weakness. Perhaps this feeling was enlarged by the repeated warnings of my judges that, if I continued to defy them, inevitably I would fall sick.

In any event, it was with this rather ambivalent approach that I answered a summons to the interrogation room, to find two five-pound Red Cross parcels awaiting me. Agnes explained that I was free to accept them and then added, with obvious distaste, that I would not even be required to sign a receipt for their delivery. This pathetic little girl, who had lost her femininity to fanaticism, had been involved in the long arguments over the "poisoned" cookies. It pained her, after that experience, to waive the rule requiring a signed receipt. Apparently, however, she had been told that I must be induced to take the parcels regardless of the regulations.

This little gesture was enough to warn me that the authorities had a particular reason for giving me my own parcels. At that time I rejected them firmly, if somewhat reluctantly. But I decided to work out a strategy to obtain some of the items, and particularly the vitamin tablets which I had seen listed on the front of each package, as a means of keeping up my strength for the long fight ahead.

On this premise, and as a test, I finally began to accept a few cans of tuna and similar food, while also demanding some of the vitamins, which had been removed from the packages. Nothing happened to my demands, of course, but the authorities seemed pleased whenever I took something from one of my own parcels. They called me frequently to the interrogation room for this purpose and behaved, at first, as if they expected nothing in return.

After this had gone on for about two weeks, the interrogator (judge) summoned me for a particularly severe lecture and a new demand that I sign a confession. When I receded again into silence, he barked hoarsely, "I suppose you would like to continue receiving your food parcels. Well—"

"Never mind," I snapped. "I know what you are going to say. I want nothing more from the packages."

"Oh, we will continue to give them to you," the judge said, more affably. "But in return you should be willing to cooperate with us."

"I will not accept any more packages as long as you are trying to bribe me."

But the authorities were as persistent in this matter as on the question of a confession. When I was transferred to the bucket of blood, the packages followed. I was summoned regularly to the interrogation room, where the parcels which already had accumulated would be spread out.

"What would you like today?" the interpreter invariably would ask.

"Nothing."

This became a ritual, unvarying and predictable, which I soon found to be both strengthening and weakening. At that period, and particularly after being threatened with a death sentence, I cherished nothing more than the opportunity to react conversely to every communist move. Although in each instance the interpreter or the judge made an effort to hide reaction, I knew that this tactic annoyed and disturbed the authorities. It gave me new confidence to be able to do this.

But the fall of 1955 also marked the first of China's great crop failures, and the general shortage of food was projected even into our bug-spattered cell. The quantity of rice permitted during our two daily meals decreased, and vegetables were virtually eliminated, except for wormy potatoes. The afternoon meal usually was bitter, watery soup, made from boiled eggplant. It was so unpalatable that even half-starved prisoners had difficulty getting it down, but we still had to finish all our food to avoid a tongue-lashing for wasting the people's work.

The authorities used this unwholesome situation in their continual attempt to wear down the captives. Theoretically, a man could obtain seconds, and sometimes his reward, after the soup, would be a can of thick, mushy rice mixed with melon—truly a feast. But he might also get a second can of eggplant liquid. Many times, my cellmates gambled and lost. They often became so sick from the additional soup that they had to rush to the barrel and give up their whole meal.

In this situation the recurrent sight of my own food parcels was tantalizing, as the authorities had expected. It required conscious will to resist them and even at this late date to avoid considering the authorities as halfway decent for offering them.

I was determined, however, to continue to refuse the parcels until assured they would not be used for bribery. Many times, in order to accomplish this, I had to sit in my stinking cell and remember all the bloody atrocities which the communists had practiced against my friends. This, perhaps, is an unnatural attitude for a priest, and I found it so in my case. But without the conscious and frequently revitalized belief that I was dealing with implacable, ruthless enemies, I fear I would not have been able to withstand the lure of their smiles and their gifts. Such is the power of persuasion.

The authorities were by no means finished with this gambit. Upon leaving Massenet prison, I was permitted one of my rare baths. More impressively, I was allowed to stay alone in the large concrete tub where bathing was by squad, in the infrequent periods when it was permitted. Comparatively sanitary, I was transferred to Ward Road jail, where promptly I was given my first decent shave in twenty-eight months and a haircut that skinned me to the skull. Thus "softened," I was greeted in the new jail by a contact man of doubtful ability but undeniable charm.

I called him Johnny, because the name was so inappropriate. He had little of the swiftness or the plain honesty customarily associated with that name. Instead, in his youth, a year or so out of college, he already had become an amateur bunco artist, communist style. Short and stocky, with heavy horn-rimmed glasses shielding bulging eyes, he carried on his intrigues in a manner of nervous moistness. Johnny's sole task, it seemed, was to persuade me to accept my packages.

He did this by demonstrating obsequious politeness and by a patter of sweet talk. On my first day at Ward Road jail, he called me from the cell to a sort of reception room in the cellblock, invited me with extreme politeness to sit down and proceeded to tell me how fortunate I was. It developed that I was lucky to have him as a friend, because he would make sure that my packages were delivered. As he talked, he constantly mopped his moon face with a handkerchief and, I thought, he looked over his shoulder with unnecessary frequency.

Johnny annoyed me, because he was so patently insincere, and I set out to use him to get me the vitamins I definitely needed. I insisted that I would accept the parcels only under certain conditions and only if they contained the medicine.

"But," Johnny insisted, "the food is easier to obtain than the vitamins, because they are still being tested by our laboratories, to see if they are safe."

"Or perhaps the vitamins already have disappeared."

"What do you mean?" Johnny asked.

"I have seen the parcels many times and have inspected

them," I answered, "and I have noticed that many things are missing."

"What is missing?" said Johnny, with a touch of belligerency.

"Some of the food is gone and all the cigarettes, as well as the matches and the opening keys for some of the canned fish."

"I know nothing about this."

Johnny was learning bureaucratic obedience skillfully but, like his superiors, he could neither make a decision nor react properly to unexpected circumstances.

"You are a liar," I said, mildly but firmly. I used the Mandarin expression, "ni pu lao shih," which literally means a man that is not only dishonest but completely lacking in character. The phrase was an insult of some import, and Johnny plainly disliked it. But he could do nothing, because he was under simple and direct orders to win my confidence.

My purpose was to keep this rather unpleasant youngster on the defensive and to lay the groundwork for the old communist trick of making a number of impossible demands in order to get what I really wanted. Before accepting the packages, I told him, I would need written assurances from the judges that the food would not be used to pressure me into a confession; this was a condition, like many others, which I knew was unacceptable. Johnny took the insults and the inflated demands with an attempt at nonchalance, then told me he would investigate.

The immediate result was that I was called again to the interrogation room and told once more to select what I wanted from an extensive array of parcels. When I refused again, because the vitamins were missing, Johnny insisted that I inventory the parcels and affirm the contents. By now the parcels averaged eleven pounds, or five kilograms, and contained items ranging from canned fish to cookies and jelly.

During these sessions it gave me considerable satisfaction to sit on the floor, spread out the contents of each package and carefully check them against the master list of contents printed on the wrapper. Feeling like a supermarket clerk, I managed to take an unconscionable length of time during inventory, thus delaying my return to the fetid cell. Invariably, some item would be missing, particularly the vitamins for which I was constantly watching, and this gave me the chance to complain, loudly and bitterly. Some things apparently were taken on orders from the authorities, but I had no doubt that others fell to covetous minor officials, despite the state's insistence upon the honesty of its bureaucrats. In each case the package had been carefully repacked, and the omissions could be detected only by close checking.

This, too, became an inflexible ritual, providing some of the comic relief that had become so necessary to my well-being. The interpreters always knew that I would refuse the parcels, and they also knew I would find some reason to complain about them. Still they attempted each time to display some measure of surprise, while promising the inevitable and usually unproductive investigation. Their discomfort became humorous to me, perhaps because by this time any deviation from the grimness of the environment struck my prison-dulled wits as humorous. But there also was real comedy in each scene: a scrawny prisoner being coaxed by his jailers to accept his own food.

If the authorities recognized this irony, they suppressed their feelings. Instead, with implacable faith in the final results of brainwashing, they continued the same routine with the packages, over and over again. The issue was sufficiently important for them to keep Johnny continually on this assignment, although the results hardly commended his abilities. The more they insisted the more it became evident they had a definite purpose in mind. Otherwise, the reaction would be to say no more about the parcels, after my initial refusals, and to dispose of them elsewhere.

For one complete year this byplay over the Red Cross packages became a constant undertone for my relations with the authorities. The central theme always was to persuade me to accept communist benevolence. Periodically, the authorities added a few other overtures of their own, such as the bath, haircut, and shave, the increased food during my stay in Ward Road jail hospital, the mail from home and the welcome moments of exercise in the fresh air. Of these concessions, the food parcels clearly were the most important. They also were offered more consistently than other "kindnesses," perhaps because they cost the authorities nothing. In any case, the pattern showed that my own food was being used to counterbalance and to reinforce the heightened pressures of intimidation which, all through this period, were maintained against me.

These pressures began in the summer of 1955 when I was confined for the second time in a discussion group cell at South City jail. By that time, apparently, I was supposed to have been softened sufficiently by verbal threats and the hours of standing at attention to accept some of the promise of salvation held out by the slogans mouthed by my cellmates. The communists have unflagging faith in the effectiveness of these discussion groups to influence the waverer. They demonstrated this in the Korean prison camps, as they had earlier by making public self-criticism obligatory for every group in the massive Chinese society.

When this failed again in my case, I was thrown into the splotched cell at Massenet, to face one grim climax in the campaign of intimidation—the threat of execution. This was followed quickly by the official notification to me that the Geneva agreement had been signed, with the implied promise of my impending freedom. After a month of that uncertainty I was sent to the regular prison section of Ward Road jail and confined with a single cellmate. He conducted another of the vituperative anti-American attacks which had punctuated my prison life. After eleven days of his insults, I was considered ready for a second climax in the campaign of intimidation, on October 31, 1955.

At dawn on that day the guard told me to dress in my "best clothes," a euphemism if ever there was one. My sole garment was a black, padded Chinese gown, which I had shortened halfway to the knees to make it more suitable for cell life.

During one of the infrequent periods when we had been given sewing equipment, I had "hemmed" the gown by turning the bottom half inch to the outside at an uneven angle, looping it together with hurried, wide stitches. The cotton padding was sifting through, and I looked like a rather sloppy ragpicker, except that the authorities had given me a shave.

With my arms handcuffed behind me, I was led to a jeep and again driven into the heart of Shanghai. It was a Sunday and the Feast Day of Christ the King, a Catholic holy day of sufficient importance for the communists to recognize and, I thought, to use against me as a date for some significant event. We drove quickly through the city and soon entered a compound of squat, grimy buildings, identified by a huge sign in Chinese characters: "The People's Court of the Sixth District of Shanghai."

The guards took me to a small, dirty anteroom and plunked me on a plain bench. Twenty minutes later Agnes entered the room with ill-disguised triumph. "Do you know why you are here?" she asked. I ignored this bromidic question and continued silent.

"Today," said Agnes, with a smirk in her voice, "we are going to settle your case." She used the phrase "ch'u li," a communist term implying that the outcome can only be bad

—torture, a long prison term, or even execution. Agnes mouthed it as if she knew that the verdict would be severe and welcomed the idea. When I continued to ignore her, she finally left, with a little snarl of anger.

But Agnes had supplied precisely the right note to create doubt and uncertainty. I sat there alone for several more hours reviewing the last few months. The range of treatment, from simulated kindness to severe threat, had been unnerving and confusing, as it was designed to be. I could not know what to expect from this long-overdue appearance before a formal court, so naturally I anticipated the worst. Perversely, this only made me more determined to conduct myself with continued defiance, regardless of what transpired in the courtroom. Yet I could not escape the final tyranny of uncertainty, the powerful desire for a quick settlement of my case, so that at last I would know my fate. In all this period of new introspection I never thought of the Geneva agreement nor drew any confidence from it.

Finally, the guards took me up a dirty, twisting stairway to another bare anteroom just outside the courtroom. We were under the command of a sort of female top sergeant, a squat, iron-jawed woman of uncertain age who ordered the soldiers around as brusquely as she ordered me. She seemed to be relatively high in the hierarchy, perhaps ranking just below the judges, and the peasant-guards promptly obeyed her commands. I christened her Dora in my mind.

While we waited once more, I could hear the murmur of voices and the shuffle of feet in the courtroom. Dora nervously peeked through a small window in the door, then brusquely told the guard to remove my handcuffs. "Be sure you watch your behavior in the People's Court," she testily told me, standing in front of me with exaggerated erectness. At that moment, she looked like a young girl impersonating a school-teacher, with owlish horn-rimmed glasses and braided hair wound around her head.

The murmuring continued beyond the door, as if a secret conference were under way. But, for some reason, I expected a public trial before a crowded courtroom. I spent the next few minutes quickly reviewing the strategy I had planned. This was the big scene in the long drama, and I wanted to play my part so that anyone present would know I had not changed and that I still did not consider myself a criminal. But the spectators' benches were empty and only the officials and a few soldiers were present. Two soldiers pushed me to an old-fashioned dock in the center of the rather large room and, in European fashion, I remained standing throughout the proceedings. Six feet above me, three judges, including one woman, peered down from their raised bench. The prosecutor and his assistants sat behind a plain table at one side of the bench and Dora, as translator, sat across from them. There was, of course, no defense attorney. The room was dirty and typically drab, and it seemed as though the People's Court was sitting in the interior of a neglected warehouse.

The senior judge rapped his gavel, then stared at me through narrow, steel-rimmed glasses. Aged and thin, he looked like a woodcut of a Chinese scholar, except for his fiery eyes. "Why are you standing in the dock today?" he began, in a rasping voice. This was the usual signal for the prisoner to confess his crimes and humbly beg the court for mercy.

"I am an innocent Catholic priest persecuted because of my religion," I said, feeling confident and calm once more.

All three judges banged their gavels and roared their disapproval. A number of soldiers rushed to the dock and yelled for me to show more respect for the court.

"I have heard of your imperialist outlook," the chief judge said sharply. "I warn you that if you do not change your attitude you will be dealt with most severely. This court is not bound by the decadent traditions of your law."

The prosecutor then read the charges against me, and I learned for the first time what they were. My crime was spreading rumors and slander, because I had said that the people's government was persecuting the Catholic Church and opposed all religion. The charges supposedly were proved by reading statements allegedly taken from other priests who had been imprisoned at the same time.

When I demanded testimony from live witnesses, the court erupted into another uproar and once more I was commanded to show proper respect. The chief judge delivered a ten-minute lecture in which he again warned me that the sentence would be severe unless I changed my attitude. "Now, how do you plead?" he concluded.

As I began my same old denial, the judge motioned impatiently for silence. Then he summoned the state's one "witness," a pathetic little man who had been the janitor in the seminary where I had lived before imprisonment, when the communists captured Shanghai. He had quickly joined them, and frequently had denounced all the priests.

Now he was brought to the center of the room and placed alongside the dock. In a sharp, birdlike voice, he identified me and said I had confided my secret plans to him because he was a good Catholic (which he decidedly was not). He testified that I had told him to spread the rumor among Catholic Chinese that, in answer to prayer, the country was going to be delivered from the communists. Furthermore, he said, I had told him that Chinese Nationalist commando units had landed near Shanghai for this purpose. Finally, he accused me of ridiculing the Chinese communist effort in the Korean War by saying that the "volunteers" sent there were only cannon fodder.

This was the total "evidence." The senior judge peered at

me again and asked, "How do you plead now?"

"Everything he said is false," I replied.

"Your stubbornness will cost you dearly," the judge snapped. "This is the People's Court."

When I remained silent, the judges retired to consider their verdict. They returned in about ten minutes, solemnly reconvened the court and, at the end of a long statement, the chief judge pronounced me guilty.

"Because of your serious crime, spreading rumors, and because of your imperialistic, defiant attitude toward the representatives of the people's government," he said, "you are hereby sentenced to three years in prison."

I cannot deny that I was surprised and pleased, for I had prepared myself for a much worse penalty. Actually, I felt as if I had won the battle, even though I realized that the authorities could keep me imprisoned for a far longer period if they so desired. But the sentence implied that even such an arbitrary court could find no justification for harsher treatment, and this meant that I had successfully resisted every effort to entrap me during imprisonment. My greatest satisfaction, however, came from the belief that I had shown no sign of weakening, not even at the end. If, as I half-expected, the authorities had hidden some of my students in the courtroom, they could see I had not changed my defiance.

As the guards took me back into the anteroom, Dora walked over to me. In a rather awkward attempt to appear cooperative, she asked if I had any questions about the verdict. When I answered negatively, she continued to press me.

"Are you sure you have nothing to ask?" she said. "After all, you are not accustomed to our law."

"It was perfectly clear to me."

Dora tried a few more approaches in an almost comic effort to change from a top sergeant into a helpful ally. Finally, she reverted to brusqueness and ordered the guards to handcuff me and take me back to jail. The maneuver was transparent. The authorities wanted me to ask such questions as whether the sentence could be appealed or whether it included the time already served, so that I would show them a weakness they could work upon in the future. Furthermore, this prodding was designed to create in my mind hope of imminent release, for even a prisoner's faintest hope was exploitable.

Back in jail, the only change was a temporary suspension of interrogation or any immediate efforts to force me into a confession. But the authorities were by no means through with me, and I expected more concerted pressures when the time suited them. There was no reason to regard the jail sentence as necessarily final nor to place any trust in the possibility that it might include the two years and four months I had served already. The only course for me was to wait out my fate with undiminished resolution and awareness.

My obnoxious cellmate continued his endless anti-American tirade, to my infuriated silence. Johnny fluttered around almost every day, urging me once more to accept the food parcels. At this point the regular rations were uniformly bad, skimpy and undernourishing. My periods of weakness were more frequent and more prolonged, and inevitably they left me dispirited. Once again I had to fight consciously and deliberately against hopelessness. The surest way was to remind myself continually that my own private war with communism continued without abatement and that the stakes were as important, or more so, as on the first day of "hostilities."

The authorities let me simmer under these conditions for nearly three weeks without making another move. Then Johnny informed me that I could have the vitamins if I accepted two of my eleven-pound Red Cross parcels. Hiding my elation I agreed, for my minimum terms had been observed and I sorely felt the need for extra nourishment. At the time, I considered this as a victory, but it developed that the authorities had a much more deliberate purpose in mind than was immediately apparent.

When the packages were given to me in the cell, I reached first for two little bottles identified as vitamin medicine. One contained small thin wafers, while the second was half filled with amber liquid. They were labeled "Pabulum Vitae," which can be translated from the Latin as "Food of Life." The labels further described the contents as "a time-tried nutriment to supply the deficiencies in the diet of those who are deprived of their normal vital minerals." The manufacturer was the Domini Corporation, Los Gatos, California. Dosage: One wafer and one teaspoonful of the liquid before eating.

Intrigued by these instructions, but not particularly alerted, I opened the wafers and found, to my disgust, that they were only thin, nickel-sized slices of sugar candy. I suspected at once that the authorities had removed the legitimate vitamins for this pallid substitute. Suspiciously, I turned to the liquid, which obviously had been opened before, because half of it was gone. It was in a medicine bottle with a glass stopper which had been sealed with wax. Scraping away the wax with an old toothbrush, I removed the stopper and sniffed.

The odor was pleasing, if somewhat unidentifiable. I tasted it once, then again. It was Mass wine! For a moment I sat on the cell floor trembling with such excitement that I almost dropped the bottle. Quickly, I inspected the candy wafers and found that thin slices of altar bread, for offering Mass, had been packed between each two pieces of candy. Finally, I turned over the stopper, and it was a miniature chalice, an inch tall.

There are no words to describe the glory of that moment. For me, the greatest punishment inflicted by the communists was the brutal attempt to suppress my religion. I had not said Mass nor received Holy Communion for 888 days. I knew the

precise total, for above everything else I had marked this time on my mental calendar. No one but a priest, perhaps, can fully realize the significance of that deprivation. Suffice it to say that, if we priests drew greater strength than the average prisoner from our religion, we also had this deeper vulnerability for despair; and this could not be completely eliminated through mental prayer alone. With two little bottles in my hand, I was reborn that morning, while my cellmate mouthed his foul and meaningless deprecations against "American imperialists."

My first impulse was to say Mass immediately, but this involved a peculiar and unacceptable risk. It was reasonably evident that the communist authorities had detected the "vitamins" for what they were and had a particular purpose in giving them to me. Obviously, they expected me to offer Mass, but it was doubtful if they would punish me for doing so, even if I were caught, in view of their past reluctance to become involved in a religious controversy. This, however, did not guarantee the behavior of my unpleasant cellmate or the guard if they discovered that I was practicing a religion they had been taught to hate. I had to avoid giving them any chance to desecrate the Blessed Sacrament.

So I waited eagerly until the next morning when I expected that my cellmate would be called upstairs, as usual, to report on me. When we rose at dawn, I covertly prepared everything to begin the service as soon as my companion left. But he just sat there, insulting me, all morning—and all afternoon—while my impatience became almost uncontrollable. The authorities never did summon him that day, although he regularly left the cell every day afterward, as had been the practice previously.

Finally, in the early evening, the usual propaganda broadcast came booming into our cell from an outside loudspeaker. My companion turned to it with his customary attention and

a typical running commentary of approval. I could curb my impatience no longer, so I decided to risk saying a Mass. Facing the wall, with my back to the other man, I began the ceremony.

Toward the end, the propaganda broadcast suddenly ceased, and the cell was momentarily silent. "What are you doing?" my companion suddenly asked.

"Shut up!" I replied. "I'm taking my vitamins."

"Let me see," he answered, shuffling his feet, as if to rise.

"Leave me alone," I barked, so strongly that he made no move to come over to me. Quickly, I finished the Mass and disposed of the bottles and two little strips of handkerchiefs which I had used for an altarcloth and to wipe the chalice.

The moment passed, and nothing more was said. But I realized the explosive potentialities of the situation. After my blessing, the wine and the altar bread were sacred. Any attempt by my cellmate to touch them or to throw them to the floor, as he might do in fanatic anger, would have been an unpardonable sin. Quite literally, I would fight to the death to protect them.

Therefore, I could not risk any further chance of interruption, as a matter of both faith and practicality. It was not improbable that the authorities gave me these materials in the hope that an incident would arise, so that my religion could be insulted "spontaneously" and I could be punished further, not as a priest but, perhaps, for the heinous crime of assaulting a guard or a fellow prisoner.

Thereafter, I waited until my cellmate began snoring and the guard's footsteps had pounded away, and then I would say Mass in the heavy darkness just before midnight, while lying on the floor. After sleeping for an hour or so, I would awaken and say a second Mass for the following day. Although I drew great strength and consolation from these moments, they also became a heavy strain. I could never be sure that the guard

would not burst in on me or that my cellmate would remain asleep. Like a gambler or a combat soldier, I counted the odds after each successful service and wondered if my luck would hold. It did, fortunately, and I was able to say forty-one Masses before the wine and wafers gave out.

It was during this period that I was summoned again to the interrogation room and invited to inspect the factory districts of Shanghai. "You will find them most interesting," the judge said affably. "I fear that you are not familiar with all that we have done during the past two years, and you should know about this before you go home."

"When am I going home?"

"Now," the judge continued, oblivious to the question, "we have a number of modern textile mills around Shanghai that you should see. If you show the proper interest, I can also send you across the country to North China and Man-churia, to see our steel mills. That will take you out of the cell for a few weeks."

"These are communist factories?"

"Of course," the judge said.

"Well, you are a communist. You go see them."

The rebuff, of course, did not halt his efforts to send me on a factory tour. There was little doubt in my mind that the purpose was to propagandize the visit. Whenever he raised the subject, I refused abruptly, but he only became more insistent. Finally and inevitably, the issue came back to the question of communist benevolence.

"You are still receiving your food parcels?" the judge asked.

"No," I replied, "I refused the package today because you have removed the vitamins again. I am out of vitamins, and I need them."

"Oh, that is too bad," the judge said. "I know how much you prize the vitamins."

"When may I have them again?"

"When will you start on your trip to the factories?"

"I am not going to visit the factories."

"Ah, well," the judge said, "I am sorry about the vitamins."

The judge was merely going through the motions of trying to persuade me by words to take the factory trip, and the manipulation of the vitamins also was intended only as a secondary influence. By this time I had already been transferred to the hospital of Ward Road jail, to be near the one-shift ministrations of the maniac Wu. The transfer meant that the authorities had decided that benevolence alone would not break me, so they turned on the madman again. This subtle use of suggested force suited that period, because the authorities had decided to release me soon and probably had determined the date. They did not want to leave any marks of physical punishment that would be visible to the outside world. Yet their determination to maintain the last possible turn of pressure was emphasized by the later policy of adding the daily screeching of the second maniac to my environment.

In retrospect it is evident that the communists had a number of reasons for their long campaign over the Red Cross parcels, none of them actually benevolent. Having decided to release me, they devoted the last six months to a "fattening up" process, so that I would appear physically fit as well as unscarred. I had lost between twenty and thirty pounds, too much to regain completely under prison conditions. The diet of three meals daily in the prison hospital evidently was intended to prevent me from losing more. The authorities saw a cost-free source of supplemental food in the imported packages, so they never abandoned their attempts to get me to accept them. Finally, for a month after my eventual release from prison—on May 10, 1956—I was confined with other freed priests under house arrest, where the fattening process was accelerated, with more nourishing rations from the communists and more Red Cross parcels.

The manner in which the authorities carried out this effort was most revealing. Even though it was necessary to preserve their face, the added food never was given without strings. The communists attempted until the last to win my cooperation through gratitude, using the food parcels as bait. For this they deliberately perpetuated doubt and uncertainty over release, so that any kindness they showed toward the end of imprisonment would appear great, because I did not know that the end was so near.

Moreover, they manipulated the "vitamins" directly for this purpose. The minimum reason for allowing one supply of Mass materials—which other priests also received—clearly was to create an added sense of hope and gratitude, for further use. The authorities frequently had told me, through the planted gossip of cell informers, that they believed we priests were praying only for our own deliverance. Apparently, they could not understand that we were, in fact, praying for the salvation of the Chinese people, with no regard for our own fate. With their distorted view of prayer, however, the communists permitted the Masses to be said in the expectation that false hope and confidence would be raised so strongly that, when destroyed by the withholding of further "vitamins," the individual would turn in despair toward cooperation.

This denouement illustrated most clearly the unbridgeable chasm between American psychology and that of the Chinese communists. From the American view, my case indeed was settled with the formal, face-saving prison term of three years, leaving eight months to be actually served. Everything occurring afterward would be anticlimactic and irrelevant. With this attitude, it is possible to see how the average prisoner might even accept the invitation to visit the factories, on the mistaken premise that no harm could be done, since his case was finished and he would soon be gone.

But my case was by no means finished for the communists They had not won, since I had refused to confess, and for them nothing is completed without a communist victory. Therefore, instead of marking the case settled—as they claimed or as American authorities might do—they actually put it into the most active phase. The only limitation was the injunction from higher authorities that I should be released in a number of months, unmarked and relatively healthy. So, while they fed me comparatively well, prison officials used accelerated pressure, from screeching maniacs to vitamins, in an intensified effort to break me or to gain some propaganda advantage up until the very end of my imprisonment.

This persistence, this willingness to use every possible device for their central purposes underscored the implacable determination of the Chinese communists to win. The authorities were driven by both communist ideology and the Chinese sense of face. Under this twin lash they were ready to pounce on any last-minute mistake I might make. Yet the conditions of my release were predetermined, so I was relatively safe from further reprisal as long as I fought back within the limits of their attack and did not enlarge the battle area by, say, a physical assault on a guard.

In these circumstances, and after five weeks of house arrest, I was taken with Father Thomas Phillips, S.J., one of the five confined to the house, to the office of Ward Road jail on the muggy evening of June 15, 1956. The brisk Chinese officer grunted for us to come to his desk. He shoved forward two batches of identification papers and demanded that we sign them. Four soldiers hovered in the background, and a dejected array of baggage sat on the floor. Our total possessions were there, some of them newly retrieved from our church, in a rusty footlocker, a battered wardrobe trunk and two suitcases.

The officer glared warily at me while we read the legal

214

forms. Written in Chinese, they were bulky and contained the usual quest for detail, down to names, professions and health conditions of grandparents. What caught my eye, however, were the answers written by the authorities in spaces for identifying the two of us. Phillips was described as an "international spy." I was a "rumor-spreading saboteur."

I slapped my paper down on the desk. "I won't sign this!" I yelled, with deliberate loudness.

"You must sign it," the officer replied, attempting to contain himself, "or you will not be released."

"Well, I won't sign it. I am not a criminal, and you know it." Phillips was equally adamant but, being a milder man by nature, he merely laid his paper on the desk. Without need for consultation we both knew that our signatures now would give the communists the confessions that had eluded them for so long. It did not matter whether the authorities believed these ridiculous charges or whether they had written them into the record solely for ulterior reasons. Our signatures would be propagandized as proof of "American imperialism," and three years' resistance would be wiped out. In reality, then, this was a last-minute trap.

"I can do nothing," the officer said, in mock resignation.

"Very well," I replied. "Take me back to the cell."

Ignoring me, the officer turned to Phillips and, speaking softly, insisted that the documents were mere formalities which he needed to complete the records of our cases.

"We are not criminals," I broke in, drowning out the official's explanation. "We will sign nothing."

"Hao, hao, hao!" the officer said with abrupt impatience, meaning "okay." He thrust the papers back toward us and added, "You can take these without signing, but you will be breaking the law and you will be held responsible." Evidently he had been instructed to get us out as swiftly as possible, for otherwise he would not have abandoned the fight so quickly.

"We can go now?"

The officer nodded wearily. "You will find your new address on the form," he said.

Quickly I glanced through the sheaf of papers. "You have made a mistake," I said. "This is not the address of our church."

"Of course not. You cannot go back to your church. Go to the place assigned to you, and be sure to report to the police within forty-eight hours."

Phillips calmly asked for more information, but the officer turned back to his desk and ostentatiously began riffling through his papers.

"I will not go!" I shouted, with a fresh burst of assumed anger. "This sounds like a propaganda trap, to use us to justify communist control of the church. I will not go. Take me back to the cell."

The officer impatiently slammed his hand on the desk and barked an order. The four soldiers suddenly converged on us, pushed us out of the office, across a courtyard and into the street, outside of the jail. Our possessions were deposited at our feet. Then the great iron gates of Ward Road jail clanged shut. We had been thrown out of jail.

We stood there momentarily, chuckling at this comic finale, while a soft rain washed down. Passers-by soon stopped to stare at us, and we must have been a strange sight; with our shaved heads and oversized grimy white pants and our quiet laughter. We were the first foreigners released inside Red China, instead of being quietly deported, and the first prisoners ejected by the communist authorities.

Soon an apologetic, embarrassed Chinese approached us and identified himself as the guide appointed by the authorities to show us our new quarters. His embarrassment indicated that he was a renegade priest, cooperating with the communists, and I became doubly suspicious that the new house meant further attempts by the authorities to put us in the hands of a Peking-appointed "bishop." We had learned a short time before that Bishop Ignatius Kung, the last legitimate head of the Church, and about fifty Chinese priests had been arrested in a final communist offensive against holdout Catholic authorities.

After considerable argument with the guide, conducted to the amusement of street throngs, we finally accompanied him to our new quarters. We found that it was a small house, which the authorities had confiscated when they expelled the Belgian priests who had previously occupied it. After two weeks of freedom we boarded a ship for Hong Kong on July 4 —a little more than three years after my capture.

The Communists had fought to the end to obtain a confession, and I have no doubt that during these final seven weeks they were ready to pounce upon any indiscretion that might have helped them in this campaign. When I finally left Shanghai I felt that I had won a significant victory, for there was no doubt in my mind that the primary purpose of my imprisonment had been to obtain an admission of my "crimes." The reason springs deeply from the nature of communism and its ruthless war against its "enemies."

Chapter ten

IMPORTANCE
OF CONFESSIONS

THE COMMUNISTS HAVE DECLARED IMPLA-
cable war against all who oppose them. This is, they
say, "a struggle for life and death," or, more appropriately,
in literal Chinese: a "you-die-I-live struggle." * The list of
"enemies" is long and includes every social class, every individual and every nation that might stand in the way of permanent Communist Party power. The "imperialists" are in the
forefront, because they have been assigned a unique role both
in dogma and in the power politics of Peking's effort to enslave the world's largest nation.

In this struggle, the "confessions" of prisoners, both Chi-

---

* *People's Daily*, Peking, Sept. 28, 1959, p. 2. Another oft-repeated expression is "se ti" meaning "enemies till death," that is, all who persist in opposing communism must die.

nese and foreign, constitute a vital and necessary weapon for communist leaders. Far from being the unbelievable lies with which Americans sometimes regard them, the confessions of germ warfare continue to be a major propaganda asset for Peking and Moscow. Those who have confessed to being spies or imperialists not only contributed to communist propaganda but provided a necessary stimulus for the spread of communist ideology itself.

Briefly, the communists teach that bitter war will be fought continually by forces attempting to prevent the "inevitable" historic development of the world along patterns predicted by Marx. Internally, the theory is, the "capitalists" will not yield power voluntarily, but will fight to hold it or to regain it, until they are overwhelmed by superior force. The proletariat—the working class, led always by the Communist Party —must fight constantly on behalf of the people against this opposition of the bourgeoisie, or the capitalists. Otherwise the "utopia" of the "new society" cannot be created.

This remains the basic theory within Communist China, as in all communist nations, long after Peking has demonstrated its capacity to rule the country without any important *organized* internal opposition. Its authority rests upon power and eternal vigilance against the rise of a hostile force with challenging strength. But Peking also has made a continual effort to win popular support by identifying itself as the champion of the people and their defender against capitalist counterattack.

The "show trials" early in the regime were designed, among other purposes, to prove that the communist authorities are "good" and "just" and that they are besieged by "evil" enemies. Prisoners were paraded through the streets, instead of being quietly shot, to establish this concept. Much of the domestic brainwashing of the Chinese people has been devoted to the theme that the capitalists are planning to destroy the "people's government" and will not rest until they do so.

This idea needs continual rejuvenation from a source more convincing than overt propaganda. So communist newspapers periodically credit the people, rather than the police or army, for capturing "notorious counter-revolutionaries." Common criminals, imprisoned for robbery and similar offenses, frequently are identified as "running dogs" of the capitalists and made to admit this "crime," rather than their actual offenses. Many more methods are used, but the most important, of course, is the apparently genuine "confession" of a non-criminal prisoner, particularly a man of standing, that he is guilty of these alleged crimes.

If this perpetual conflict is to be identified as a basic factor of domestic life in any communist country, it is both logical and necessary to create a greater external menace. So communist dogma pictures "imperialism" as an international force, seeking to maintain its control over nations, as the bourgeoisie is presumed to be fighting for domestic power in every country. A huge body of theory has grown around Lenin's thesis, that imperialism is the last stage of decaying capitalism before it develops into the socialism predicted by Marx. Imperialism will fight bitterly to avoid this development, the communists teach, and will use all its power to maintain its hold over colonies and to seize new colonies. The communists also cling to the idea that capitalism cannot survive without cheap industrial raw materials from "downtrodden" colonial possessions.

Most of these ideas, like much of basic communism, have been disproved by events. Undeterred, communist theoreticians have evolved new theories of colonialism to justify their discredited basic assumptions. Even though less than one per cent of the world's people now remain under noncommunist colonial control, for instance, the communists insist that their basic views of imperialism remain valid. Indeed, they must maintain this position or admit that Marx's "inevitable" laws of history are wrong. Consequently, they insist that the European powers, having given independence to their colonies, are seeking to enslave them again through "neocolonialism" establishing control through financial investment and trade or by arms.

Moreover, since 1946, the communists have concentrated upon a multibillion-dollar effort to portray the United States as the greatest and most dangerous "imperialist" power. The basic handbook for all communists, *Fundamentals of Marxism-Leninism,* puts it this way: "Although the United States does not formally and legally possess a single important colony, it is, in fact, the biggest colonial power today." * The communists contend this "American imperialism" is being practiced through economic investments, foreign aid, the maintenance of U.S. bases abroad, the establishment of anticommunist defense alliances and other means.

The fight for complete national independence, according to this theory, is as deadly and as prolonged as the effort to eliminate domestic capitalists. Once again, the communists contend that independence, political freedom and economic "utopia" can be secured only through the revolutionary activities of the proletariat—led inevitably by the communist party. "Socialism," says the communist handbook, "has to be built in the face of bitter resistance from the imperialist camp, which exerts every effort to crush the socialist countries." And, at another point, it adds: "The replacement of capitalism by socialism is not possible through evolutionary development. It takes place by revolution, by a revolutionary leap . . ." † This is the foundation for the so-called "wars

---

* P. 306. These sentiments are echoed by Mao Tse-tung; e.g., "Imperialism and All Reactionaries Are Paper Tigers," a compilation of sayings from 1940 to 1958, *People's Daily,* Peking, Oct. 31, 1958, pp. 1 & 2.

† *Op. cit.,* p. 314.

of national liberation," which the communists now are vigorously trying to foment throughout the world.

The type of doubletalk often appears meaningless to Americans and, too frequently, it is dismissed as nonsense. But it is deadly serious to dedicated communists and to communist leaders, whose power depends upon it. Moreover, this dogma has been unaffected by what some commentators seem to regard as the growing sophistication of Soviet Russia or by its diplomatic negotiations with the West. The theoreticians have taken care to make sure that the basic theories remain unchanged by such maneuvers as Soviet Premier Khrushchev's campaign for "peaceful co-existence" with the western powers.

A definitive explanation of "co-existence" was made in a statement issued after a Moscow meeting of representatives from 81 communist parties in late 1960. "Peaceful co-existence of states," the statement said, "does not imply renunciation of the class struggle as the revisionists claim. The co-existence of states with different social systems is a form of class struggle between socialism and capitalism. In conditions of peaceful co-existence favorable opportunities are provided for the development of the class struggle in the capitalist countries and the national liberation movement of the peoples of the colonial and dependent countries. In their turn, the successes of the revolutionary class and national liberation struggle promote peaceful co-existence." The statement also had this to say: "International developments in recent years have furnished many new proofs of the fact that U.S. imperialism is the chief bulwark of world reaction and an international gendarme, that it has become an enemy of the peoples of the whole world."

Although life in Russia has changed considerably under Khrushchev, this concept of capitalist attack is nurtured as strongly there as in all other communist countries. The Russians continually are saturated with charges against "western imperialists" and warned against "plots" and "spies." Khrushchev admitted grave agricultural deficiencies in 1962, for example, but told his people he could not divert funds to buy tractors, because more arms were necessary. At the same time, the flexibility of tactics under communist ideology permitted him to talk simultaneously of "co-existence" with the West and of its constant threat to attack the communist nations.

For many reasons, Red China often has sounded even more belligerent about the dangers from "imperialism." It has been necessary to maintain and enlarge this alleged external threat in order to retain control over more than 600 million individualistic people, and to press them into more and more sacrifices. Moreover, Peking suffers a continual loss of face through its inability to "liberate" Formosa. The Chinese Communists continually claim that attack is imminent or that large numbers of agents from the Nationalist Chinese Kuomintang Party are infiltrating the country. In all this, of course, the Kuomintang is pictured as merely the tool of the United States, so that the actual charge is: The United States is preparing to invade the mainland!

Whether the Chinese Communist leaders believe their own propaganda or not, imperialism has become a basic charge and counter charge, even in high party levels. It is not uncommon to see articles in the official press denouncing party members, even in the "leading core," for showing the results of exposure to the influence of "imperialism and of foreign and home reactionary forces." * When freedom of speech was permitted briefly, during the "Hundred Flowers" campaign of 1957, critics of the regime and of Marxism were condemned and forced to apologize or sent to jail. Many prominent intellectuals and some high government officials

---

* Cf. *New China News Agency*, September 28, 1962, "Communiqué of the Tenth Plenary Session of the Eighth Central Committee."

were "exposed" as "spies," "imperialists" and "Kuomintang agents."

Chinese theoreticians, of course, constantly stress anti-imperialism, often in amazingly violent terms. One writer, for instance, emphasized the need to eliminate "capitalist influence" upon children under seven years of age in advocating a new educational program a few years ago. The child of this age, he said, "needs to know socialist science, he needs to know the distinction between the enemy and ourselves, the distinction between good and bad." Furthermore, he added: "Let the tots know the happiness of Socialism, the poverty of workers' children in capitalist countries, the miseries of life in colonial and semi-colonial lands, the effects of imperialist invasion on colonial countries, and most important of all, let them understand that American imperialism is the worst enemy of the peoples of the world." *

Mao Tse-tung has established the official line for the imperialist concept and has provided the theoretical base for making it into a self-perpetuating means of extending communist party power. "It must be understood," he said, in 1957, "that the hidden counter-revolutionaries still at large will not take it lying down, but will certainly seize every opportunity to make trouble, and that the United States imperialists and the Chiang Kai-shek clique are constantly sending in secret agents to carry on wrecking activities.

"Even when all the counter-revolutionaries in existence have been routed out, new ones may emerge. If we drop our guard we shall be badly fooled and suffer for it severely. Wherever counter-revolutionaries are found making trouble, they should be rooted out with a firm hand . . ." †

More than domestic control and internal brainwashing

---

* *People's Daily*, Peking, May 19, 1960, p. 7.

† Mao Tse-tung, "On the Correct Handling of Contradictions Among the People," *New China News Agency*, June 18, 1957.

are involved in this steady drumbeat over western "imperialism." The communists never tire of reminding themselves that, by their figures, the communist nations have grown from eight per cent to thirty-five per cent of the world's population since before World War I. Their figures show that thirty-seven per cent live in the newly-freed colonial nations, eighteen per cent in "imperialist-capitalist" societies, with the remainder presumably in unclassifiable societies.

The communist drive for world power is concentrated upon this thirty-seven per cent in the freed colonial nations. These nations reached independence with varying degrees of enmity for their former overlords, and the communists found that their most effective channel of approach was through their alleged opposition to "imperialism." The enormity of communist aggression and imperialism remain only improperly understood. In various subtle ways, the communists also have sought to turn racial and color hatreds into acceptance of their theories on imperialism. These appeals appear to have been far more effective for the communists than any widespread acceptance or understanding of Marxism-Leninism.

The Marxist concept of western "imperialism," then, is deadly serious, and anyone involved in it cannot escape the importance of his role. The whole idea is so involved and complex that the communists rely upon simple explanations and readily understandable "proof" to make the point credible to the millions of people involved. They have many ways of doing this, but obviously a signed confession from a prisoner is the most effective. A Chinese who claims that he was a "spy" paid by Kuomintang agents, acting for the Americans, can influence large numbers of his countrymen, when his confession is published, even though few of them may know him personally. The impact naturally is far greater when a foreigner, and particularly an American, "confesses" that he is an "imperialist" or a "spy" or a "warmonger" or any of the other charges so frequently made.

This is why the communist authorities spent so much time on me, and all their other prisoners, in the attempt to get what would appear to be a voluntary "confession." A statement in my own handwriting, widely published, most certainly would have affected the Chinese students and friends who trusted me and my promise not to sign any such document. If, as likely, the authorities would have followed this by immediate publication of photographs, showing me without marks of torture or brutality, the impact would have been even greater. The natural reaction would have been to assume that I had been convinced of my own country's wrongdoing by logical persuasion, not through torture. Why, then, should any student of mine hold out longer?

From this, it is easy to see why brainwashing has been developed into such a semi-scientific practice, with tens of thousands of men and women involved in applying it to prisoners and to the general public. Massive use of force tends to become self-defeating, either in individual or mass cases. The mental enslavement of people is much surer, even if it does not reach the ultimate stage of creating completely controlled reflexes. The authorities relied upon cooperative prisoners to supply the "proof" needed to make such charges as "imperialism" and "counter-revolution" convincing to large masses of Chinese people. Having accepted these "confessions," the masses then would be more receptive to further brainwashing and less liable to resist the regime.

As a propaganda measure, the importance of an American "confession" can hardly be over-emphasized. Published in the man's own handwriting, it receives the same credibility in Africa as in China. If he admits being an "imperialist," for instance, he "proves" the basic claim that the communists are trying to establish, and agents always will be on hand to make this point. Moreover, in their attack on the poorly-educated peoples, the communists make no effort to explain their entire ideology or to make it intelligible. They depend, instead, upon proving one of their claims, then using this to justify everything else they say. This is one reason for heavy emphasis upon western imperialism among peoples already prejudiced against it. If they can be led to believe that the Americans themselves confess being imperialists, many millions may be more willing to listen to the next communist claim, however implausible it might be.

So it is not surprising that the communists are still relying upon the "confessions" of germ warfare, received from Korean prisoners ten years ago, to prove a great mass of propaganda spread throughout the world. In the intervening ten years, communist propagandists continually have referred to these confessions, so that millions know of them. It is no longer necessary to publish the actual documents.

With this in mind, the purpose of a speech delivered in Tokyo in August, 1962, becomes clearer. The occasion was the communist-controlled "World Conference Against Atomic and Hydrogen Bombs," and the speech was given by Pa Chin, leader of the Chinese Communist delegation. The Peking *New China News Agency* gave this version of one section: "U.S. imperialism conducted germ warfare in Korea in 1952," he (Pa) went on. "That is why the Koreans called the U.S. aggressor troops 'civilized brutes'. The U.S. troops who killed several million Koreans are still running amuck in the southern part of Korea— The Kennedy administration . . . recently conducted chemical warfare in South Vietnam. Large numbers of South Vietnamese are being slaughtered with U.S. chemical weapons at this moment when the conference is in session," he said. This report was broadcast in English throughout Asia and Europe.

A short time earlier, the Pyongyang Radio of North Korea stepped up the brainwashing of its own people on this same point. A domestic broadcast claimed that the United States was conducting extensive research on "a small new-type bacteriological weapon." Then it added: "During the Korean war for three years the U.S. cannibals massacred Koreans by all sorts of bestial methods. . . . For the purpose of wiping out the Korean people, they even waged bacteriological warfare without hesitation by spreading various kinds of insects laden with epidemic germs."

The communists, no doubt, would have made these same charges repeatedly throughout the years, even if they had failed to obtain any American "confessions." The point is that the American statements gave them far more credibility than any unsubstantiated claims would have. And so the recollection of these "confessions" is counted upon to give new meaning to fresh charges.

The individual American prisoner who comes under brainwashing, then, is involved in a new and infinitely more important phase of the cold war than if he remained on the battlefield or in his own church. A soldier in combat is one man in a unit, and he can neither win nor lose the engagement by himself, under ordinary conditions. Once in prison, however, he becomes, in effect, the entire army; and the stake is world opinion, not an isolated hill. Moreover, what he says may be important for a decade and may affect millions of people.

This is the answer to the question I have been asked numerous times: "What difference does it make if an American admits something that no one in the United States would believe?"

Chapter eleven

TOTAL VICTORY
IS POSSIBLE

THE ESSENCE OF BRAINWASHING, AS I HAVE tried to show, is the attempt to induce an artificial psychosis in each prisoner. It is this ultimate purpose which distinguishes the communist treatment of captives from that of other dictatorial aggressors.

The communists seek to distort the individual prisoner's instincts and to pervert such debilitating emotions as guilt, despair, fear, loneliness, uncertainty. When basic mistreatment has aroused these emotions sufficiently, the exhaustive lectures, the subtle traps and the moments of "kindness" are invoked, to prey upon the victim's heightened suggestibility. Many of these measures have been used before in the penology of dictatorships, but the combination of communist techniques is new. The Chinese have built this into a pseudo science by patient experimentation.

But the effectiveness of brainwashing depends, in the end, entirely upon the reaction of the individual prisoner himself. As my experience shows, there is nothing magical in any of the communists' methods or in the total technique itself. Success depends upon creating the desired response within the prisoner. Without this, brainwashing is bound to fail. In other words, the communists have created an elaborate system for the purpose of forcing the prisoner to defeat himself.

This does not result solely from the most appalling of the techniques—torture, brutality, inhuman treatment—because these have been practiced time and again by conquerors, without producing any significant degree of cooperation from their captives. Neither does it result primarily from any persuasiveness of Marxism-Leninism. The communists have no high rate of Party recruitment from their jails, nor have they attempted to achieve one. These pressures are important, but they are fully effective only in combination with the other influences directed against the prisoner's will and his mind.

The main battle area, then, is located within each captive's deep inner self—his strengths and weaknesses, his hopes and aspirations, his disillusionments. The communists probe relentlessly for weaknesses from the past to turn against the prisoner. They maintain constant prison pressures to produce new weaknesses. Therefore, the only adequate defense is absolute resistance to both of these attacks; resolute opposition to every communist maneuver.

There is, unfortunately, no easy way to wage this fight. It would be unwise to underestimate the practical ability, the cleverness and the ruthlessness of the men who conduct brainwashing. The technique has been developed after thousands of hours of experimentation upon innumerable human guinea pigs. But neither should brainwashing be overestimated as a tactic of unfailing efficiency or mystique. Although the communists boast that they can break any man, they have been proved wrong in numerous cases. The American prisoners who successfully resisted in Korea, among others, demonstrated the hollowness of the communist boast. The technique has weaknesses, as my story illustrates, and so do the men who apply it. Brainwashing can be overcome.

For anyone involved in it, brainwashing *must* be overcome. The stakes, quite candidly, are the prisoner's mental well-being in prison and, perhaps, for many years after release. He must fight or be lost, for the communists have devised a merciless process; a conflict to the finish. Every American coming under this diabolical influence, furthermore, becomes involved in the battle against communism, whether he likes it or not, as long as he remains in communist hands. I say, again, that he is transformed by circumstances into a one-man army, and he must defend his own front. The communists do not tolerate neutrals.

The American prisoner, moreover, becomes a special target because he is an American, and his nationality places on him a particular obligation to fight back; for the consequences of his defeat are great. Most Americans undergoing this ordeal have shown that their patriotism, their love of country and their love of freedom are sufficient motivations to make this fight, once they understand the consequences of capitulation. Even if this were not so, however, the need for resistance would be equally strong. The most abject, beaten men I have ever seen were those who collaborated with the communists, sometimes against their will, and who lived on in guilt and self-hatred.

Each man subjected to brainwashing will respond in his own way, of course, and with his own peculiar heritage of strength and weakness. No infallible set of rules or guidelines can be devised to cover every situation or to provide emergency strength. But I am convinced that, in this situation, knowledge, quite literally, is power. Knowing the enemy and his techniques is a very considerable part of the conflict.

In the past, I fear, many of those who succumbed to brainwashing made their major mistakes before they were captured. That is, they had decided that the technique was unbeatable, or that they could protect themselves in prison by cooperation, or that a confession would be unimportant. With this attitude, the preliminary goals of brainwashing already were achieved by the time the communists started work on their victims. Every man liable to communist capture, I believe, should know fully in advance what he faces in communist hands and what the significance of his actions will be.

This means he should be prepared for all the tricks of entrapment, all the subtle persuasions and all the planned shifts of approach and manner which characterize the communist tactics. Strong men, as well as the weak, have been trapped into cooperation or self-revelation because they were unaware, beforehand, of the communist methods. The prisoner should know, too, that for the communists prison treatment is a part of their implacable war, and moments of apparent kindness and benevolence are only methods of waging that war. Since the conflict for them will continue until their victory or defeat and since the communist man is obliged by dogma to follow Party discipline, regardless of his own thoughts, there is no time for a temporary truce or for periods of genuine friendship. Finally, the endless patience and diligence which the authorities displayed in an effort to get a confession from me underline the importance they attach to each captive American. No American is so unimportant that he can be excluded from their master effort to use him for propaganda or for other advantage.

The prisoner should also realize that he can do nothing to improve his position with the communists. The treatment of the Chinese "progressives" who shared some of my worst days was one of many proved signs that the communists have only contempt for those they intimidate successfully. Therefore, cooperation with the authorities is no guaranty of safety or of improved conditions. Quite frequently, it only leads to worse treatment and almost invariably it produces further pressures for more and more collaboration.

Consequently, the essential issue is not whether the captive can gain by cooperating, but how much he will lose. Frequently, his immediate treatment deteriorates as the result of his efforts to improve it by capitulation. Since collaboration also almost invariably produces self-guilt, the loss is fundamental to the prisoner; for guilt is the primary emotion upon which the authorities seek to capitalize. Moreover, the first mistake cannot easily be rectified, and the prisoner can hardly ever resist further collaboration after giving in originally. The initial conflict between the prisoner and his captors can be decisive over this fundamental issue of cooperation.

For his own well-being, as well as for reasons of ideology and patriotism, the captive then must begin his ordeal with the inflexible determination to avoid any type of cooperation. There is no room for bargaining on this issue, and no feasible way for the prisoner to size up his captors first and then determine his attitude toward their inevitable overtures. Unless he is prepared to remain adamant, he stands to risk the entire battle for the control of his mind. He has no choice but to oppose the authorities, if only mentally, every step of the way.

The importance of a prior knowledge of communist tactics was emphasized by one of the Americans released in Laos during August, 1962. John McMorrow of Brooklyn, a civilian helicopter mechanic, was jailed for sixteen months by the procommunist Pathet Lao army. Upon his return to the United States he told me that he was helped greatly during this ordeal by the instruction given to him beforehand by a former prisoner of the North Vietnamese communists.

Having decided on the necessity for resistance, the prisoner must fight on two fronts. The first is the area of his own past, the accumulated weaknesses or uncertainties which the communists try to exploit. The past cannot be changed, but each man can hold grimly, as I tried to do, to its strengthening and comforting experiences. The second battlefront involves the individual's reaction to his immediate circumstances and to the new pressures of imprisonment. The prisoner's adjustment to this challenge depends considerably upon the kind of man he is or can make himself be.

The strongest, quite naturally, will be those with an abiding faith—in their family, their country, their religion. They may be imbued with patriotism and dedicated to the preservation of the American system against tyranny. They may be primarily concerned with survival, so that they can rejoin their families. Or they may be men determined to protect their human identity and their souls from the attacks against them. Whatever the faith, it should, in most cases, enable the prisoner to identify the communists as the relentless enemy they are. And this recognition is the first step toward insulation against the entrapment as well as the threats of brainwashing. A man must have reason to fight.

The Korean War showed, unfortunately, that not all the Americans sent into combat against the communists had a faith to sustain them during captivity. It may have been too late, by that time, for the dispossessed to acquire strong convictions. No one had taught them what they needed to know —the pricelessness of human dignity and freedom; the universality of the communist menace; the poverty of a man with nothing in which to believe. They had gone to war without realizing the importance of the conflict, and had marched off to prison without knowing that they still were at war.

Yet many of those who eventually collaborated were

tricked, not persuaded, into doing so. If they had known in advance the techniques they had to resist, the rate of cooperation might have been far less. If they had been given a faith, even a modest faith, in their own value as individuals, cooperation doubtless would have been more infrequent. I am convinced that every man of determination has the capacity to resist brainwashing if he knows what to expect and if he realizes the necessity for resistance.

In combating the attack against his mind, the prisoner must practice the deliberate and constant strengthening of every characteristic and human attribute which communist treatment seeks to weaken. I have tried to show the tactics which worked in my case, by describing them in some detail. First, by recalling the sunny and tender episodes of my life, I fought successfully against the attempt to discover and capitalize upon weaknesses and doubts from the past. Second, by driving my brain to new imagery and by keeping it constantly in motion, even to the plotting of counterstrategy, I resisted the atrophy and despair that brainwashing was designed to induce.

After the initial and basic decision to fight back, I found that a few additional mental attitudes were essential. A sense of humor, for example, became indispensable. If there is nothing funny in the sight of a grimy jail, then humor must be deliberately introduced by the mind, either from the past or through a new oblique look at the surroundings. I taught myself to chuckle inwardly at the baggy pants hiding my trembling knees and to guffaw mentally at the authorities' confusion during my fight over the cookies.

It was necessary also to abandon temporarily some of my ingrained Americanism. Instead of the gregariousness which, perhaps, is a national characteristic, I deliberately cut myself off from any group influence, as an essential measure of self-preservation. Although by training, as well as by instinct, I customarily looked for the best in men, I was obliged constantly to regard cellmates and authorities alike as enemies and to force myself deliberately into maintaining this attitude, however pleasant they attempted to be on occasion. There could be no compromise on this issue, for compromise inevitably would be fatal for me.

Neither could there be any compromise, in my mind, on the basic principles of my imprisonment and the purposes for which the authorities intended using me. I proved in my first encounter that debate with the communists was fruitless, even on Marxist lines. Beyond that, I found, there was no room to negotiate with the authorities, and no way to avoid the reality that I was caught up in a desperate struggle between freedom and slavery. The communists recognize only friends and enemies, with no middle position, and conduct their entire campaign on that premise. In this situation, there was no room for the fair-minded American characteristic of attempting to see and understand both sides. I could not admit that, even under their laws, the authorities had any justification for imprisoning me. Instead, I had to harden myself into inflexibility on this principle by insisting at every opportunity that I was imprisoned illegally and was being persecuted as a priest. Every captive must do the same, for the authorities are quick to seize on any sign of temporizing. They regard it as a glaring sign of weakness.

I found that the best defense against entrapment was complete silence, and I am convinced this is best also for the average prisoner. By this I mean avoidance of debate or any consequential conversation, particularly of an informative nature. The civilian should limit himself to the essentials, and the soldier should confine his autobiography to the routine name, rank, and serial number. This not only eliminates the risk of betraying himself, but it enables the captive to preserve strength for the difficult task of anticipating and repelling every assault on his mind and will.

But silence and passivity are not entirely enough. They sometimes lead to compromise through the accumulated frustration of a supine defense in the face of wearing harangues and insults. An experienced communist judge can word his charges so cleverly that silence can be construed as acceptance of them, particularly in front of witnesses. This is a standard technique, for instance, during the public trials of captives who refuse to confess their "crimes."

Moreover, an active attack is essential for the prisoner's well-being and is necessary for adequate resistance. I found that my own capacity to resist was strengthened immeasurably by taking the offensive, whenever a suitable opportunity arose. Silent opposition was insufficient to supply the small but necessary sense of achievement which became indispensable amid my unhuman squalor. A certain understanding of communist and Chinese psychology was necessary. As I have said, the fundamentals of this psychology can be perceived by using common sense and by familiarity with the principles of brainwashing and communist dogma. By challenging the authorities on the central issue of my false arrest, I was able to throw them off balance and to upset their plans for controlling me. They demonstrated their inability adequately to handle any reaction contrary to their expectations.

Even though my attitude might have appeared extreme to the authorities, they refrained from direct assault on me, no doubt because it was outlawed by policy. If the policy had called for torture, however, nothing could have prevented it. Perhaps my punishment was more severe because I maintained the offensive, but, if so, the results were well worth it.

None of these countermeasures against the communists are easy and none entirely free from risk. But the prisoner's choice is not between a benevolent and a harsh imprisonment. In the end, his only choice is the manner in which he survives imprisonment, in his service both to himself and to his country. A man can win only when he completes the ordeal with his own integrity unimpaired and with his mind solid and free from self-guilt. All the loneliness, the self-isolation, the self-control, the determination, the harrowing uncertainty are part of a desperate battle, in which one man is alone against a powerful and ruthless state.

The challenge of brainwashing was as great in 1962 as when I left prison six years earlier, and the technique remained standard for all communists. One of the prisoners released from Laos, Major Lawrence R. Bailey, Jr., confirmed that the same essential tactics of brainwashing were used against him during sixteen months' imprisonment. He told me of cruel isolation in a dark room; consistent interrogations by an English-speaking communist officer; constant demands for a written "confession"; periods of prolonged questioning, then days of being ignored, and—above all—the constant uncertainty about his fate. He had no assurance of release, even after the conclusion of a fourteen-nation agreement at Geneva for an armistice in hostilities and the permanent neutralization of Laos. In fact, he was not told that he would be released until several weeks after the agreement had been signed and after all organized fighting had ended. Despite the inhumanity of this treatment, which sent him home on a stretcher, Major Bailey was not tortured nor physically touched. This, no doubt, was the result of central policy, to avoid the reaction of direct physical violence.

Brainwashing is the continuation of the communist war against free men in the remote battlegrounds of prisons and war prisoner camps. It is no less deadly because guns are seldom used, because large armies are not involved, and because the mind is the target. The men who may fall under it need to know their enemy and his methods as thoroughly as they understand his battlefield tactics. They need to know their own capacities, their own strengths and weaknesses, as completely as they know rifles and hand grenades. With that knowledge they can fight as effectively and as determinedly as in the front lines. Without that knowledge, they will be unarmed for what may be the most important battle of their lives.

This is a new kind of warfare for American service men, but it is being fought on the terrain they know best—the mind and the will. I have no doubt that they can master it.